THE BEST
NATURAL FOODS
ON THE MARKET TODAY

THE BEST NATURAL FOODS
ON THE MARKET TODAY

A YUPPIE'S GUIDE TO HIPPIE FOOD
VOLUME I

Greg Hottinger, MPH, RD

HUCKLEBERRY
MOUNTAIN
PRESS

Huckleberry Mountain Press

This book is for educational purposes only. It is not intended as a substitute for medical advice. Please consult a qualified health professional for individual health and medical advice. Neither Huckleberry Mountain Press nor the author shall have any responsibility for any adverse effects arising directly or indirectly as a result of the information provided in this book.

Throughout this book, trademarked names are used. Rather than put a trademark symbol after every occurrence of a trademarked name, we use a trademark symbol after the first occurrence only. Thereafter, with no intention of infringement of the trademark, company names and products are printed with initial caps only.

Cover designed by Laura Duffy
Book designed by Desktop Miracles, Inc.
Hippie illustration by Max Werner
Printed and bound by Malloy
Cover graphic: kiwi fruit (*Actinidia deliciosa*)

Publishers' Cataloging-in-Publication
(Provided by Quality Books, Inc.)

Hottinger, Greg
    The best natural foods on the market today : a
yuppie's guide to hippie food. Volume I / Greg Hottinger.
    p.   cm.
    Includes index.
    LCCN 2004 102124
    ISBN 0–9749796–0–0

    1. Natural foods.   2. Cookery (Natural foods)
I. Title.
TX369.H68 2004   641.3'02
                           QBI04–200122

 This book is printed 85% recycled, 30% post consumer paper

www.hippiefood.com

For information about special discounts for bulk purchases,
please email specialsales@hippiefood.com

To Bill and Jane,
my wonderful parents,
for standing by me

Contents

SECTION THREE: A Closer Look at the Main Issues   159

Acknowledgements

This book was an idea for a long time until it slowly trickled its way to the surface. Without the support of many friends and colleagues, it never would have made it. I'd like to thank a few of these great folks who helped me along the way.

I have much love and gratitude for Casey Ostertag, a true friend, great writer, and wonderful support in my life over the last seven years.

Huge thanks to Jeffrey Magner, my partner in this project, for being an amazing coach and friend. Without his support, this book would have remained on my hard drive along with the others. A big hug and thanks to janeAnne Narrin for being a gift from the stars. She believed in the book before I did. Her words, both written and spoken, were invaluable. To Claudia Green for being a steadfast friend and kindred spirit. Also thanks to her boys Curtis and Colin. To Louise Massey for helping me survive grad school and beyond with humor. To Mandy Graves for listening and spawning many creative ideas. To my Asheville buds, Emma and Tim Pluta, for such warm friendship. To my masterful yoga instructor Heidi Anderson for striving to be real. To my awesome sister Lynn and her equally-awesome husband Dan and little Janie. Thanks to Chip, Becky, and Griffin Law for staying connected. To Anne and Wes Weaver and Jim and Cheryl Collins for ongoing friendships.

To Michael Scholtz, my partner in coaching weight loss at NOVO Wellness. Thanks for hanging in there along the way. Thanks to Susan Head and Stephanie Nilsen for our collaborative efforts. May there be many more!

Thanks to all the folks at the Duke University Center for Integrative Medicine for maintaining a wonderful vision of whole-person medicine. Thanks to Tracy Gaudet, Rich Liebowitz, Sam Moon, Linda Smith,

Larry Burke, and Ruth Quillian for being an awesome team and keeping an open heart (and an open mind). Thanks to the rest of the DCIM team: Jeff Brantley, Karen Gray, Cay Melges, Margo Evrenidis, Linda Duda, Kerry Little, Andrea Shaw, Jessica Psujek, Jeanne Gresko, and the others. To Marty Sullivan for opening the door for me at DCIM. To my friends and colleagues at the Duke Diet and Fitness Center, especially Franca Alphin and Michael Hamilton for showing me what a healthy work environment looks like. Ciao and grazie to Elisabetta Politi for friendship. And to Che Che Casto, the unsung heroine.

To Ron and Sue Ostertag for being great fans. And to Maggie Holmes and Tom Hamilton for showing me a glimpse of what is possible.

Thanks to Mary Trainor-Brigham for being a true blessing as an editor. And to my amazing cover designer, Laura Duffy. To Patrick Hanaway for his suggestions and support. To Lynn Horn for her design contributions. And a big thanks to Leah Joy for her creative process. To Jena Chambers for her editing input. Thanks to Max Werner for his artistic contributions. And to Del LeMond and Barry Kerrigan for putting it all together.

Finally, I'd like to thank my brother Jeff for helping me get started down the natural foods path. . . .

Introduction

In 1990, I completely changed the way I ate. It all started when I stumbled upon the book *Fit for Life* by Harvey and Marilyn Diamond. After reading it and a few more nutrition-related books, I was inspired to give up all foods made with white flour and white sugar. I also stopped eating foods that were processed and which contained preservatives. It was quite a shift. Luckily, my family members really got in to what I was doing, and we made the dietary changes together. My friends, however, thought that I had gone over the edge, and no amount of explanation seemed to shed light on my unusual food choices. As for the other people in my life . . . well, they were completely confounded with my radical departure from normalcy and quickly lumped me into the *hippie* category.

What precipitated my lifestyle change, from fast-food junkie to connoisseur of lesser known health foods, was that I was starting to learn the truth about food and health; I "woke up," so to speak. It became clear to me that my standard American diet, which appeared to be working fine for me at 24, was actually paving the way for a host of health problems down the road, most of which could be avoided.

What I discovered turned everything on its head. I wondered why the same foods that our ancestors ate for thousands of generations— called **Hippie Foods** today—could be considered a radical way to eat. What healthful benefits could possibly be derived from the modern day diet of refined flours, hydrogenated oils, and soft drinks? I could not think of any.

I was not able to buy most of my newfound foods from a supermarket near me, so I began driving long distances to go to natural food stores and food co-ops because, at the time, there were few options in North Carolina. With a shopping list in hand, I purchased weird-looking beans and grains with odd-sounding names. Having grown up in the South, I had never even heard of most of these items, but before long I was enjoying such uncommon foods as tahini and kale. As the months and years passed, I experimented with raw foods, food combining, juicing, and fasting before finally settling on my current whole-foods, Mediterranean-style fare.

I am not the only one who has changed during this last decade; the once decried **Hippie Foods** of yesterday have stepped out of the shadows and onto center stage. Part of the reason for this turn-around is that the scientific world has provided some of the answers to the food/health puzzle. Research conducted over the last few decades has transformed the field of nutrition from the study of how to make a better pound cake to the science of preventing, and in some cases *reversing*, disease.

The emerging field of Nutrition captured my attention. In 1997, after finishing graduate school and receiving my degree in Nutrition, I was asked to teach at the Duke University Diet and Fitness Center. I worked with folks who were just beginning to understand the importance of eating a healthier diet, due in part to the fact that they desperately wanted to lose weight. I enjoyed the opportunity to help these people, most of whom were highly motivated to improve their relationship to food. Despite their desire to change their food habits, their resistance to trying "healthy" and sometimes unfamiliar foods intrigued me. For example, clients would often refuse to even *taste* a dish that I made in a cooking class if it contained tofu or tempeh. I soon realized that transforming the eating habits of my clients, much less the diet of the average American, was going to be a real challenge. Media advertising and a fifty-plus year tradition of convenience food have greatly misled us. Modern-day foods, many of which are concocted in laboratories and which we think are *real* and health promoting, simply are NOT.

My most motivated clients at Duke University taught me that they might try new foods but were unsure of how to make the right changes to support their new health goals. At the same time, they were realizing that their health depended on the quality of the foods in their diets and were ready to change their buying habits. Indeed, the natural foods market has grown 20% annually since 1990, largely because of this realization. Still, adding new foods into one's daily repertoire is not easy; it requires the choice to step outside of the mainstream and, in many cases, paddle against the current. It asks us to seek out information on different foods on the market today: How are these foods raised or produced? What are their nutritional benefits? How can we make them into palatable, or dare we say delicious-tasting, meals? I began research to answer these primary questions. You are holding the result of this effort.

Section One: Getting Started briefly discusses the relationship between food and health. *Section Two: The Best Natural Foods on the Market Today* profiles thirty natural food products. Here you will find much of the information you will need on why and how to add a food to your diet. *Section Three: A Closer Look* delves into some of the hottest topics facing the food industry today. I review controversial agricultural issues, like the use of antibiotics and hormones on farm animals, and the emergence of genetic engineering and its possible impact on the food supply. I give you what I believe is useful information, such as the latest on whole-wheat, milk products, soy products, fats, and oils. And finally, you can enjoy the *Natural Foods Coupons*, the last few pages of the book that were developed with the help of the natural food companies. These have been included to make it a little easier for you to give these products a try.

I chose the subtitle, *A Yuppie's Guide to Hippie Food*, to bring just a bit of light-hearted fun to a topic that often seems too serious. Remember, before natural food stores hit the *big time*, most of us associated "healthy foods" with the Hippie movement of the 1960s. In writing this book, I acknowledge the contributions of those who stood firm for healthy food long before it was fashionable. As a result of these efforts, we now have the choice to choose foods that are simple and whole, that contain no refined flours or refined sugars, hydrogenated oils, fake fats, synthetic sweeteners, or a long list of additives. Today we can go to a store in our town and choose food that has not been doctored with hormones or antibiotics, sprayed with herbicides and pesticides, irradiated, or genetically engineered. With our purchases, we can even support the organic farmer who has expressed a commitment to preserving the soil and water so that the land can produce food for generations to come. Author Skip Stone aptly describes how hippies were the pioneers of the natural foods movement:

> *Health food stores and cooperatives exist now in almost every decent-sized town and city in the U.S. This is directly a result of the Hippy fondness for health, quality and freshness. Hippies helped promulgate the laws that regulate organic produce found in many states. Organic farming is now accepted as a regular practice across the country.*
>
> *Hippies helped popularize Indian food, especially curries and chapatis, dahl and basmati rice. Asian foods like tofu, soybeans, tamari, rice crackers, miso and tempeh are now part of many healthy American diets. We buy bulk foods like flour, grains, beans and nuts, sold by the pound, not prepackaged and left on supermarket shelves for years. Whole grain bakeries all over the country now offer a variety of multigrain breads which are far tastier and healthier than the traditional American white bread. Yogurt, kefir, goat milk, soy milk are all non-traditional dairy products popularized by hippies. You can thank us for all of these wonderful products being on the shelves.*
>
> — Excerpt from: *Hippies From A to Z: Their Sex, Drugs, Music and Impact on Society from the Sixties to the Present*, (HIP Publishing)

I firmly believe that eating natural food is essential for restoring and maintaining health. With this in mind, I have selected all of the products in this book based on their nutritional merit. Many of these foods are my personal favorites, and I believe they truly are the best products available today. I contacted all of the manufacturers profiled here and have not accepted any form of payment from participating companies. There are many wonderful and healthy products in a natural foods store; those presented here are only a sampling. Keep your eyes open for volume two of *The Best Natural Foods on the Market Today: A Yuppie's Guide to Hippie Food.*

Throughout the book, you'll see Huckie, a hippie who lived for a few years in the late 1960s in Haight-Ashbury. He trekked across the country in his VW van following the Grateful Dead and other bands and went to Woodstock. Along the way, he learned to prepare simple, healthy, tasty foods, and many of his favorites are found here. At the end of each section, he shares his *Hippie Wisdom* to remind you of key things to look for when choosing quality food products.

Getting Started

Understanding the relationship between diet and health makes choosing quality foods much easier. You may be surprised when you stop and consider how foods in the supermarket have changed in the last few generations. How do these changes affect you and your health? This section briefly discusses these issues, as well as strategies that can help you make healthier food a higher priority in your diet.

- *What's In (or Not In) Your Food?*
- *Healthy Food: What's It Worth?*

What's In (or Not In) Your Food?

Prior to the food processing explosion of the early 20th century, most food choices were wholesome; the issues of depleted soils, synthetic fats, genetically engineered foods, and preservatives were non-existent. People ate foods that were raised on a local farm. As our way of life changed, however, we became less connected to the farm and to knowing where food really came from. We became dependent on the supermarket, fast-food places, and packaged foods, and while these changes were convenient, we started paying the price with steady weight gain, diabetes, and other health problems until we began to see that the foods we were eating deserved our careful attention. Our bodies have relied on locally-gathered foods for nourishment for thousands of years, so it isn't any wonder that our choices for overly-processed foods have created a serious healthcare crisis. Sure, people are living longer than ever, but if we look around, we notice that many of us are surviving and not thriving.

Are our modern ailments related to nutrients we are not getting from our diet, or could they be the result of unhealthy substances added to our food? Or possibly both? It is time for us to look into the real value of a **whole-foods diet**, one consisting of whole grains, whole grain breads, whole grain cereals, beans, vegetables, fruits, lean meats, dairy products, and nuts and seeds. Certainly, the health revolution that has driven the growth of the natural foods market indicates a growing awareness of a very simple idea: A whole-foods diet helps the body restore health and function better.

How this basic concept actually works is still largely a mystery to modern-day scientists. Yes, it's true that we have a large amount of evidence to support the relationship between certain diets and health. But, when we try to understand how nutrients affect healing, or how healing by itself occurs, we have just begun to scratch the surface. One noted researcher recently said, "We think it will be a *long time* before science unravels the complexity of nutrient interactions in the relation of foods to health."[1] Most of us are unaware of this truth (Do you realize that your favorite plant foods contain *thousands* of different chemicals?). In the meantime, researchers are trying to understand the effects of more than 5,000 *phenols* like those in red wine, 700 *carotenoids* such as *lycopene* found in tomatoes, 200 *phytoestrogens* such as those in flaxseed and 100 *glucosinolates*, like *sulforaphane* in broccoli. And to make matters more complicated and confusing, researchers agree that phytochemicals (plant chemicals) often work together (synergistically), explaining why consuming isolated supplements is not as effective as eating whole foods. Imagine trying to understand all that might occur at the cellular level when we assimilate the chemicals in a single clove of garlic, which include:

1,2-(prop-2-enyl)-disulfane, 1,2-dimercaptocyclopentane, 1,2-epithiopropane,1,3-dithiane, 1-hexanol, 1-methyl-1,2-(prop-2-enyl)-disulfane, 1-methyl-2-(prop-2-enyl)-disulfane, prop-2-enyl), 1-methyl-3-trisulfane, 2,3,4-trithiapentane, 2,5-dimethyl-tetrahydrothiophene, 2-methyl-benzaldehyde, 2-propen-1-ol, 2-vinyl-4h-1,3-dithiin, 3,5-diethyl-1,2,4-trithiolane, 3-methyl-2-cyclopentene-1-thione, 3-vinyl-4h-1,2-dithiin, 4-methyl-5-vinylthiazole, 5-butyl-cysteine-sulfoxide, adenosine, ajoene, alanine, allicin, alliin, allistatin-I, allistatin-II, allixin, allyl disulfide, allyl-methyl-disulfide, allyl-methyl-trisulfide, allyl-propyl-disulfide, alpha-phellandrene, alpha-prostaglandin-F-1, alpha-prostaglandin-F-2, alpha-tocopherol, aluminum, aniline, arachidonic acid, arginine, ascorbic acid, ash, aspartic acid, beta-carotene, beta-phellandrene, beta-tocopherol, biotin, boron, caffeic acid, calcium, calcium-oxalate, choline, chromium, cis-ajoene, citral, cobalt, copper, cycloalliin, cystine, desoxyribonuclease, diallyl disulfide, diayll sulfide, diayll tetrasulfide, diallyl trisulfide, digalactosyl-diglyceride, dimethyl-difuran, dimethyl L-disulfide, dimethyl-L-sulfide, dimethyl-sulfide, dimethyl-trisulfide, eicosapentanoic acid, ferulic acid, fiber, folacin, fructose, gamma-L-glutamyl-isoleucine, gamma-L-glutamyl-L-leucine, gamma-L-glutamyl-methionine, gamma-L-glutamyl-S-allyl-cysteine, gamma-L-glutamyl-S-allyl-mercapto-cysteine, gamma-L-glutamyl-S-beta-carboxy-beta-methyl-ethyl-cysteinyl-glycine, gamma-L-glutamyl-S-methyl-L-cysteine-sulfoxide, gamma-L-glutamyl-S-propyl-cysteine, germanium, gibberellin-A-3, gibberellin-A-7, glucose, glutamic acid, glutathione, glycerol sulfoquinovoside, glycine, guanosine, hexa-1,5-dienyl-trisulfide, hexokinase, histidine, iodine, iron, isobutyl-isothiocyanate, isoleucine, leucine, linalol, lysine, magnesium, manganese, methionine, methyl-allyl-sulfide, methyl-allyl-trisulfide, methyl-propyl-disulfide, monogalactosyl-diglyceride, myrosinase, niacin, nickel, nicotinic acid, P-coumaric acid, peroxidase, phenylalanine, phosphatidyl-choline, phosphatidyl-ethanolamine, phosphatidyl-inositol, phosphatidyl-serine, phosphorus, potassium, proline, prop-2-enyl-disulfane, propene, propenethiol, prostaglandin-A-1, prostaglandin-A-2, prostaglandin-B-1, prostaglandin-B-2, prostaglandin-E-1, prostaglandin-E-2, protodegalactotigonin, protoeruboside-B, pseudocoridinine-A, pseudocoridinine-B, quercetin, raffinose, riboflavin, S-(2-carboxy-propyl)-glutathione, S-allo-mercapto-cysteine, S-allyl-cysteine, S-allyl-cysteine-sulfoxide, S-ethyl-cysteine-sulfoxide, S-methyl-cysteine, S-methyl-cysteine-sulfoxide, S-methyl-L-cysteine-sulfoxide, S-propenyl-cysteine, S-propenyl-cysteine-sulfoxide, saponin, sativoside-B-1, scordine, scordinin-A, scordinin-A-1, scordinin-A-2, scordinin-B, scordinine-A-3, scorodose, selenium, serine, silicon, sodium, sucrose, thiamacornine, thiamin, threonine, tin, trans-1-propenyl-methyl-disulfide, trans-ajoene, trans-S-(propenyl-1-yl)-cysteine-disulfide, tryptophan, tyrosinase, tyrosine, uranium, valine, vitamin U, zinc[2]

Nobody understands what really happens inside your body when you digest a meal. And yet, somehow, after millions of years of adapting to the compounds in plants and in wild animal foods, your body knows precisely how to metabolize them. That is, except for the recent and unrecognizable chemical additives: hydrogenated oils, synthetic sweeteners, and preservatives. These foods are not native species and present challenges for the body to overcome and which, over time, can cause serious and chronic health problems.

While optimal health requires regular balance in other areas such as physical activity, emotional well-being, and a sense of purpose, we have lulled ourselves into thinking that our diet somehow does not relate to our health. Sure, we have come to see that our food choices can prevent heart disease and cancer, but how many of us associate what we choose to eat with the thousands of smaller aches, pains, and ailments like heartburn, indigestion, insomnia, skin conditions, allergies, and headaches? Common lore blames these problems on genetics, stress, or bad luck. But after having coped with health problems for years with pills, many people around the world are curing themselves by simply switching to a whole-foods diet. These folks avoid processed foods completely for a period of time and by doing so, give the body a chance to heal itself with a steady supply of the right nutrients.

Healthy eating requires us to take a closer look at the question: *"What's in (or not in) our food?"* The following sections provide the facts you'll need about natural foods to better understand the issues. Sometimes learning this information is uncomfortable. Sometimes you may wish that you really didn't know any better. My intention in presenting this book isn't to over-state the issues. Instead, my aim is to provide you with accurate information, thereby empowering you to make healthier choices for yourself and your family.

Healthy Food: What's It Worth?

"Outrageous Prices!" You probably have uttered this phrase when talking about healthful foods. It is true that a shopping cart of natural foods costs more than ordinary supermarket foods. That is why I encourage my clients to understand the reasons for the price differences. Ultimately, you will pay more for natural food—or anything else—if you perceive that it offers you more *value*. Natural food products are distinguished from supermarket foods in the ways that they are made, and these differences are important in helping you maintain your health. If you are able to re-frame the cost issue to see it as value *added*, and you identify ways to keep a lid on the overall food budget, you will be able to meet the "What's It Worth?" challenge.

Most of us have an inaccurate view of the *real* cost to produce food. There are many reasons why our supermarket foods are relatively inexpensive. The shift from small farms to large farming operations in the past fifty years has boosted the overall supply of food. There is greater emphasis today on *quantity* over *quality* with the reliance on chemicals to boost production, machinery to farm expansive tracts of land, and underpaid migrant workers to carry much of the remaining burden. Warehousing, refrigeration, and round-the-clock trucking have made distribution incredibly efficient. Furthermore, the use of preservatives and processing technology increases the shelf life of many supermarket foods. Finally, costs are contained directly by the U.S. government which spends billions of dollars each year subsidizing the agriculture industry. As a result, our food costs are the lowest in the world. It is estimated that the average American family spends roughly 10% of its disposable income on food. Europeans spend up to 20%, whereas those living in developing countries such as India, spend as much as 50%–80% of disposable income on food.

Anyone who has garden experience knows the challenges of growing food. The obstacles include bad weather conditions, insects, animals, and poor growing seasons. The technological advancements put into use to manage these obstacles undoubtedly have increased our food production, but the very real health concerns associated with synthetic fertilizers, pesticides, herbicides, antibiotics, and hormones are the reasons why people are seeking products from the natural foods market.

If you choose natural food products, you must factor in the extra care involved in its production. When you do this, you will not be shocked by the prices. Quality food costs more. That should not be news to us. After all, advertisements constantly preach the message of getting our money's worth. We are encouraged to buy luxury automobiles, spiffy clothing, superior housing, and all kinds of leisure items. We readily spend $50 on a restaurant meal, so why do we resist buying a $2 head of broccoli? That broccoli has REAL value!

Remember too that organically produced foods and other natural food products typically are grown on a smaller scale. These foods are not enhanced with synthetic chemicals or antibiotics. Natural foods are raised less intensively and are not preserved in an unhealthy way. Being unprocessed, many natural foods have a much shorter shelf-life so that the price of these foods accurately reflects the *true cost* of producing quality foods.

Understanding why natural foods are more expensive does not change their price, but it can help shift your perception of the cost difference. The natural foods market attracts individuals who care about quality foods and see them as a necessity whether they earn a six-figure income or not. Use these strategies to help you make healthy food a higher priority.

Strategies

• "I'm worth it."

Self-care includes eating foods that are health-promoting. You may think that spending more money and time on yourself is selfish, but lose that thinking fast! Consider the analogy of the heart: It pumps blood to the lungs to pick up oxygen. The heart then pumps the blood back to itself before nourishing the rest of the body. Is the heart *selfish* for feeding itself first, or is there some wisdom in all of this?

• **Pay now or pay later—with interest.**

Your health today and tomorrow depends on the *quality* of foods that you choose to eat consistently. The costs incurred later in life are not just financial. Costs are measured in terms of suffering, pain, and loss of functioning. Many people maintain excellent health, save thousands of dollars each year, and avoid the need for costly medications just by choosing a healthy diet.

• **Consider preparing wonderful home-cooked meals more often.**

The extra cost of natural foods can be off-set in part by preparing more foods at home. Cutting out just a few restaurant bills makes a noticeable difference on the plus side of your natural foods budget. Are you one of those folks who will fork over $3 for a drink at a theater or restaurant but resists paying $3 for organic juice at a natural food store?

• **Choose less-processed foods and more bulk foods.**

Many higher-ticket items in the diet—including those found in a natural foods market—are processed foods. Offset the cost of adding natural foods to your diet by selecting more whole-food items including those sold in the bulk section. For example, a box of breakfast cereal can easily exceed $4 whereas an equal amount of oatmeal sold in bulk may cost only $2. Brown rice sold in bulk costs less than a packaged rice product.

• **"Donate" to sustainable farmers.**

If you typically give to charitable causes, consider your extra expense of natural foods a donation to a healthier way of producing food! Many organic farmers today make an extra effort because they are committed to producing a better product that benefits you. They need and deserve financial support. By regularly buying quality organic foods, you are strengthening these farmers' livelihoods. As more farmers practice organic farming, natural foods will become less expensive.

- **Prioritize.**

Consider selecting the specific items/products to buy from the natural foods store in place of those that are known to contain the most chemical residues. This is a great place to start (see Section Three: *Organic Farming*).

The Best Natural Foods on the Market Today

In this section, thirty different food products are presented. For each food category, one specific brand is discussed in detail. You will notice that several poultry producers are profiled. The reason is that no single producer currently provides poultry to every natural foods store in the country.

The food categories presented are:

Chicken	Almond Butter	Salsa
Eggs	Cereal	Spelt Flour
Milk	Juice	Tempeh
Soy Milk	Soup	Tahini
Almond Milk	Crackers	Quinoa
Yogurt	Tortillas	Soy Sauce Alternative
Soy Yogurt	Cheese Alternative	Nutritional Yeast
Cottage Cheese	Beans	Flax Oil
Butter Alternative	Ginger Ale	Miso
Bread	Tortilla Chips	Dulse

Chicken

Chicken is the most popular source of animal protein in America today. On average, each of us consumes more than 75 pounds of chicken every year.[3] Our intake has nearly doubled since 1970, an increase driven largely by the popularity of fried chicken and other breaded chicken products. The many best-selling high-protein diets have also fueled this explosive growth. Unfortunately, changes in the chicken industry over the last few decades (to accommodate the high demand for this popular food) have adversely affected the *quality* of chicken meat found in regular supermarkets and restaurants.

The days of free-running chickens pecking at worms and scratching in the compost pile on the farm are a distant reality. Today's chickens are bred and raised to reach the supermarket as quickly as possible. Instead of farms, the chicken industry uses warehouse-like structures to provide the living environment for as many as 100,000 chickens at a time. These chickens are fed rendered meat scraps including hog and cattle byproducts, and waste products including their own manure.

DID YOU KNOW?

The modern chicken reaches market weight in 45 days. In 1950, chickens were raised 75 days before going to market (and they weighed 40% less!)

The end result of these large-scale, "efficient" operations is chicken meat that is relatively inexpensive to the consumer—that is, if the consumer is only considering the monetary measure. The cost is *enormous* when we factor in our health.

Eighty percent of supermarket broiler chickens are infected with the bacteria *Campylobacter* and twenty percent with *Salmonella*.[4] Overcrowding and unsanitary conditions create a more stressful environment and greater disease rates among poultry, necessitating the use of antibiotics. The Union of Concerned Scientists estimates that *seventy percent* of all antibiotics produced in the U.S. are fed to animals, and the majority of these drugs are used to promote growth and *prevent* disease. A survey of 1,000 Americans found that 48% are unaware that conventional chickens are fed a diet that contains antibiotics to help prevent flock-destroying diseases.[5] Approximately half of the antibiotics used to keep chickens "healthy" are identical to those used to treat humans. The over-use of these antibiotics creates bacteria that are more drug resistant. The Center for Disease Control is studying resistant *Campylobacter* strains that make people sick for three days longer than normal and increase the need for hospitalization.[6] The Food & Drug Administration (FDA) has issued warnings and is requesting that pharmaceutical companies avoid selling certain drugs to the poultry industry (see Section Three: *Antibiotics*).

While health authorities say that the solution to foodborne illnesses is greater care when handling raw chicken and thorough cooking, it makes better sense to try to produce healthier birds by simply feeding them a quality diet without waste products, and providing them with a cleaner and less-stressful environment. How would you know if your chicken was raised with these extra measures? One common designation, used effectively to market chicken products, is the term "free-range."

What does *free-range* really mean?

Found on labels and menus, it does NOT paint an accurate and consistent picture. The USDA has defined "free-range" loosely as having outdoor access for "an undetermined period each day." Consumers are not told whether the chicken is fed a natural diet or one that includes animal products, waste products, and/or antibiotics. "Free-range" also does not indicate anything about the quality of the outdoor space or the number of chickens that share that space. Another misnomer is the use of the term "hormone-free" on chicken labels. The FDA banned the use of any growth-promoting hormones on chickens decades ago (see Section Three: *Hormones*) making this label accurate but misleading when used to sell chicken on this claim alone.

Fortunately, there are chicken producers that have taken extra steps to raise a healthier chicken. These farmers understand the real costs associated with intensive poultry operations, and they are choosing a better way to bring chickens to the marketplace. Without question, these extra measures increase the cost of chicken meat, but many consumers gladly pay the difference for a healthier bird, especially when they learn the truth about how chickens are raised (see Section One: *Healthy Food: What's It Worth?*).

Let's take a look at four of the leading chicken producers in the natural foods market today.

About Bell & Evans®

Bell & Evans Company has been producing quality poultry products since 1890. The highest quality chicken they raise today, labeled the Excellent Chicken® is fed a 100% plant and vegetable diet, free from antibiotics. The Excellent Chicken must pass a rigorous inspection. All chickens are raised in a climate-controlled chicken house with much more space than typical within the industry. These birds get clean air, sunlight, and well-water administered through a sanitary "drip-and-sip" technology designed to prevent contamination. Bell & Evans takes cleanliness measures that prevent many diseases and eliminate the need for antibiotics. No chicken that requires medication during its life is sold as a Bell & Evans product.

All of Bell & Evans chickens are fed a wholesome diet that consists of locally-grown soy beans, enhanced with corn, and amino acids to provide more protein. The nutrition regimen includes fifteen times the recommended amount of Vitamin E to help bolster the young chick's immune system and three times the recommended amount of the fat-soluble vitamins (A, D, E, and K) and the B-vitamins to support overall health. No artificial preservatives or non-nutritive coloring agents are used in the food supply.

Bell & Evans chickens are free to roam in spacious warehouses; however, they're not "free-range," a fact that company officials defend by saying it protects their chickens from exposure to bad weather, disease, and eating foods outside of their carefully designed plant-based diet.

The Excellent Chicken is never frozen because the company has found that consumers prefer fresh chicken. Instead, Excellent Chicken is packed loosely in ice so that the chicken never gets colder than 34° F. For more information on Bell & Evans, visit: http://www.bellandevans.com/

About Eberly Poultry®

Eberly Poultry Company still finds its home in the same rolling Pennsylvania Dutch Country where it started more than fifty years ago. Today, eighty small family farmers raise Eberly Poultry according to strict standards. In 1991, it became certified as an organic poultry processor by the Northeast Organic Farmers Association of New York (NOFA) and became Pennsylvania Certified Organic (PCO) in 1998 (see Section Three: *Organic Farming*).

All of the chickens raised by Eberly Poultry live in a natural environment with access to sunshine, fresh air, and room to move. The organically raised chickens are fed only organic grains without antibiotics or artificial ingredients. Independent inspectors regularly test Eberly Poultry chicken feed to assure that it does not contain any growth stimulants, antibiotics, animal by-products or pesticides. NOFA and PCO inspect the company's poultry farms and processing plants to ensure that the animals are treated humanely and that cleanliness regulations are being met. Unlike virtually all commercial producers, Eberly Poultry takes extra care by processing their chickens *by hand* without mechanization. For more information on Eberly Poultry, visit: http://www.eberlypoultry.com/

About Petaluma Poultry®

Petaluma Poultry Company has been raising chickens since 1969 and has demonstrated a strong commitment to producing healthy chickens. One of their products, marketed as Rocky®, was the first USDA approved free-range chicken and another was the first to carry a certified organic label. Petaluma Poultry farmers feed an antibiotic-free, plant-based diet to their birds consisting of corn and soybean meal. Chickens are raised in a spacious, low-stress environment with access to natural sunlight. It is typical for Petaluma Poultry chickens to mature for 60–70 days before being sent to market (the industry standard is 45 days). The chickens are handled humanely, and the producers who raise them practice sustainable farming methods.

Chickens that carry the Rosie® label—in addition to the aforementioned practices—have been fed a diet of 100% certified organic corn and soybean grown on soil that has been free of pesticides, herbicides, and chemical fertilizers for at least three years. Petaluma Poultry raises these chicks in accordance with the organic regulations independently verified by Oregon Tilth, a third party certifier (see Section Three: *Organic Farming*). For more information on Petaluma Poultry, visit: http://www.healthychickenchoices.com/

About MBA Poultry®

On a trip to Europe, MBA Poultry founder Mark Haskins made a culinary discovery: European chickens tasted better than those he was accustomed to eating back home. What he came to realize is that this difference is largely a result of how European chickens are processed. Instead of the water immersion process used by every major American poultry producer, Europeans use an air-chilling technique. In addition to the taste benefits, research has shown that air-chilling reduces the risk of *Salmonella* and *Campylobacter* contamination by fifty percent.[7]

MBA Poultry Company began selling the Smart Chicken® in 1998 and it is currently the only brand in the U.S. that is air-chilled. The company raises all of its chickens on a 100% vegetarian diet of corn, soybeans, and vitamins and minerals with no antibiotics. MBA Poultry also produces a USDA *certified-organic* Smart Chicken. MBA Smart Chickens are available in thirty states across the country. For more information on MBA Poultry, visit: http://www.smartchicken.com/

Taste

You're familiar with the joke, "Well, it tastes a little like chicken!" This raises a question: What does *really good* chicken taste like? I've heard many an old timer say that it's hard to find a delicious chicken today. It makes sense to me that a chicken raised in an old-fashioned way would actually taste better than the average chicken today. Results of recent competitions conducted by magazines have confirmed the suspicion that a healthier bird does in fact, taste better. In 1994, *Cook's Illustrated* magazine conducted a taste test of nine different chickens, including five premium brands and four leading supermarket brands. The panel of judges included several chefs, food critics, and restaurateurs. The results were consistent. The premium chicken brands came in first, second, third, fourth, and seventh. A Bell & Evans chicken came in first place. *The Washingtonian Magazine* conducted a blind tasting of six different brands of chickens in 1994. An Eberly Poultry chicken placed first.

Chickens fed real food (no meat scraps or waste products) and given more space produce better quality meat that is tastier and healthier to eat. Better conditions benefit the chicken, the farmer, and the consumer. Most supermarket brands are produced by intensive agriculture methods and are fed a diet that includes animal by-products and antibiotics. Ask your natural foods market for information on the chicken products they sell.

Hippie Wisdom

- Choose chicken that has been fed a healthy diet free of antibiotics,
- Choose organic chicken products when possible, and
- Investigate locally-raised chickens from your local food co-op or farmer's market. You may find a producer that raises chickens the old-fashioned way.

Outtasight Thai Chicken

1 tablespoon toasted sesame oil

1 heaping teaspoon ginger, minced

4 garlic cloves, minced

1 medium onion, chopped

2 cups carrots, chopped

2 tablespoons Bragg Liquid Aminos® (see food category: *Soy Sauce Alternative*)

1 cup water

2 teaspoons red curry paste (hot or mild)

3 medium white potatoes cut into 1-inch pieces

1 pound Bell & Evans, Eberly Poultry, Petaluma Poultry or MBA Poultry chicken breast, cleaned and cut into 1-inch pieces

1 teaspoon salt

1 cup coconut milk

½ cup chopped cilantro

1 teaspoon rice vinegar

1. Heat oil in a large skillet over medium heat. Add ginger and cook for approximately 1 minute.

2. Add garlic, onion, carrots, and Bragg Liquid Aminos. Cook for several minutes covered.

3. Add water, curry paste, potatoes, chicken, and salt. Stir until curry paste is well-dissolved. Cook for approximately 10 minutes covered.

4. Add coconut milk and cilantro. Simmer for an additional 2–3 minutes or until chicken is thoroughly cooked.

5. Add rice vinegar and serve over rice or quinoa.

Serves 4

Nutrition Analysis per Serving: 390 calories, 22 grams fat, 13 grams saturated fat*, 4 grams monounsaturated fat, 4 grams polyunsaturated fat, 29 grams protein, 24 grams carbohydrates, 5 grams fiber, 950 milligrams sodium

---

*Note: The 13 grams of saturated fat per serving is 65% of the Daily Value. If you have high cholesterol levels, make this dish with light coconut milk. More than half of the saturated fat grams in coconut are medium-chain triglycerides, a class of fats that do not significantly affect cholesterol levels. There is no solid evidence that eating coconut milk or coconut oil as part of a healthy diet raises the risk for heart disease.

Eggs

Eggs are making a comeback in the eyes of many health-conscious consumers. After decades of being labeled a villain for containing too much cholesterol, more recent evidence indicates that eggs' impact of dietary cholesterol on blood cholesterol levels is not as significant as previously thought. And there's more: All eggs are not created equal. Research shows that the nutrients in eggs vary significantly depending on the diet of the laying hen.[8] Consider our discussion of chicken and extrapolate from there. Healthier chickens lay eggs that contain higher levels of omega–3 fats which have important health benefits.

> **DID YOU KNOW?**
>
> Egg consumption dropped from more than 400 eggs per person per year in 1945 to an estimated 235 eggs in 1990. Today the average consumption is nearly 260 eggs per person.

There are farmers today who realize that they can greatly enhance the taste and quality of the eggs they produce. Gold Circle Farms® is one of the producers that is on the cutting edge.

About *Gold Circle Farms®*

Gold Circle Farms was established in 1998 with a dedication to providing nutritionally enhanced eggs from chickens that are fed an all-natural, plant-based diet. Gold Circle Farms has long known that adding nutrients to the diet of their laying hens produces nutritionally superior eggs. The addition of marine algae into the diet of the chicken results in eggs that have **eight** times the concentration of the omega–3 fat DHA as compared to a regular supermarket egg. DHA is one of the long-chain omega–3 fats also found in salmon. Research indicates that adding it to your diet may reduce your risk of dying from heart disease (see below). For more information on Gold Circle Farms, visit: http://www.goldcirclefarms.com/

Cage-Free DHA Omega–3 Eggs®

The authors of a study of more than 80,000 women concluded that one egg added to the diet each day is not likely to increase the risk of heart disease* or stroke among healthy individuals.[9] It is worth noting that this research was not even based on the consumption of DHA omega–3 eggs but on ordinary supermarket eggs. Furthermore, studies show saturated fats to be the main culprits—those found in cheese, ice cream, and butter (see Section Three: *Fats & Oils*). Take heed cheese lovers, it's the melted stuff *in* the omelet that is more likely to send your cholesterol levels soaring unlike any plate of scrambled eggs.

One effective way to help the body metabolize the cholesterol in eggs in a healthier way is to add an antioxidant-rich food to the meal. For example, whenever I eat eggs and toast in the morning, I always use a really good 100% blueberry or raspberry fruit jam. I might also eat a few strawberries or an orange. When fats and cholesterol are oxidized by free radicals, they become more dangerous to your arteries. The simple additions of these antioxidants can help prevent cholesterol from oxidization.

OMEGA–3S

A good friend of mine who suffers from arthritis was amazed when I told her about the omega–3 secret; it can ameliorate rheumatoid arthritis, Crohn's disease, psoriasis, multiple sclerosis, and more. I explained that the addition of marine algae to the laying hen's diet increases the DHA (docosahexanoic acid) content in the egg yolk from 18 mg (supermarket egg) to roughly 150 milligrams per egg. Other than the heart benefits, DHA also promotes an overall anti-inflammatory response that benefits most everyone but particularly those with inflammatory diseases. DHA might also lower your blood pressure and help reduce your risk of developing macular degeneration, depression, some cancers, and possibly Alzheimer's disease.

---

*The current American Heart Association guidelines recommend limiting daily cholesterol intake to 300 milligrams for healthy individuals (one egg contains 215 milligrams) and 200 milligrams for those with heart disease risk factors.

There is a growing body of evidence to support the relationship between DHA intake and optimal brain and eye function of infants. During the third trimester, the growing fetus derives the essential DHA fats from the mother. Research shows that higher DHA intake by the mother, even during breastfeeding, correlates to increased DHA levels in infants, and significantly higher scores in visual acuity[10] (a marker for cognitive development). The World Health Organization (WHO) has recommended DHA supplementation of infant formulas since 1994 because of the role that DHA plays in the development of the brain and retina.[11] The U.S. Food and Drug Administration approved the use of DHA in baby formula in 2001.

HOW MUCH DHA?

Health practitioners often recommend three servings (one serving = 3½ ounces) of "oily" fish (like salmon) each week which would provide roughly 1,800 milligrams DHA. The DHA amount found in four Cage-Free DHA Omega–3 eggs is equal to one fish serving. But that's not all. Each Gold Circle Farms egg also provides 20% of the recommended daily allowance for vitamin E, six times more vitamin E than a regular supermarket egg!

Eggs can be a good source of quality protein. Chickens fed a healthier diet and given room to roam (not a cage) will lay eggs that contain higher amounts of beneficial nutrients.
- Choose eggs that are raised cage-free,
- Choose eggs from chickens fed a natural diet that includes a source of omega–3s (often indicated on the label),
- Choose eggs from chickens fed an organic diet, and
- Investigate locally raised eggs from your local food co-op or farmer's market. You may find a producer that raises his chickens on a natural, organic diet.

Hippie Wisdom

Eggs-cellent! Egg Salad

4 Gold Circle Farms Cage-Free DHA Omega–3 eggs

¼ cup Nayonaise®, Vegenaise®, or Spectrum® organic mayonnaise (all natural foods products)

⅛ teaspoon salt

¼ teaspoon ground black pepper

Dash of paprika

2 tablespoons green olives, chopped (use jalapenos or pickles instead, if desired)

1 celery stalk, chopped

1 tablespoon chopped red onion (optional)

1. Place eggs in a saucepan and cover with water. Cover and bring water to a boil on high. Once water starts to boil, cook eggs for exactly five minutes.

2. Promptly remove eggs from heat, keep covered, and let eggs sit in the water for five additional minutes. Remove eggs, cool, and peel.

3. While eggs are cooking, mix mayonnaise, salt, pepper, and paprika in a large bowl.

4. Add peeled eggs and mix thoroughly with a fork.

5. Fold in the olives, celery, and onion, and mix. Refrigerate until chilled.

6. Serve with bread or crackers.

Serves 2

Nutrition Analysis per Serving: 220 calories, 13 grams fat, 2.5 grams saturated fat, 7 grams monounsaturated fat, 3 grams polyunsaturated fat, 430 milligrams cholesterol, 11 grams protein, 13 grams carbohydrates, 0 grams fiber, 820 milligrams sodium

Other Noteworthy Nutrients per Serving (DV = Daily Value):
Omega–3s (DHA) — 300 milligrams

Milk

Cow's milk has been a staple food for Americans for many, many generations. It is one of the classic farm foods. Today, however, milk consumption is on the decline despite the efforts of the dairy industry and the $100 million spent each year promoting dairy products through marketing campaigns like the "Got Milk?" ads. An increase in the number of meals eaten away from home, a smaller percentage of children in the U.S., and a steady rise in soft drink consumption have contributed to this decline.

Despite the decline in milk consumption, the $40 billion dairy industry has grown steadily in its production and distribution requirements because milk is a key ingredient in many different foods. Half of all milk consumed in the United States, for example, is in the form of cheese. What you may not realize is that the small dairy farmer is quickly being replaced by large, corporately-owned farms. From 1992 to 2002, the number of milk producers dropped from nearly 160,000 to around 90,000, a 40% decline.[12] With fewer farmers, the industry has been able to increase overall production during this time by 11% through breeding practices and the use of technology.[13] Forecasters predict that the industry will grow increasingly more concentrated. By 2020, the number of dairy farms will fall to 16,000, an 80% decline from today.[14]

> **DID YOU KNOW?**
>
> In 1945 the average person in the United States consumed 45 gallons of milk each year (41 gallons of whole milk) whereas today the consumption is less than 23 gallons (8 gallons of whole milk) each year.

Cows have been bred to produce greater and greater amounts of milk. Today, cows on average produce six to eight gallons of milk each day compared to only a gallon and a half from a cow a hundred years ago. Milk production *per cow*, even in the last decade, has increased 16%.[15] Yet despite these significant breeding advances, dairy farmers feel the unending pressure to produce even more milk to stay competitive with larger dairy operations.

One method of increasing output is to give dairy cows a hormone called bovine somatotropin (BST), also called bovine growth hormone

(BGH). Currently 15% of all cows are regularly injected with BGH, which increases milk yield by nearly a gallon per day. Approved by the Food and Drug Administration (FDA) in 1993, BGH was met with great resistance and remains highly controversial today (see Section Three: *Hormones*). There are currently no labeling guidelines requiring producers to indicate the presence of BGH in the milk that they sell.

Taking a step back, you can see that the trends of the last decade have created a lose-lose-lose situation: The dairy farmer is working harder, the cows are under more physical duress to produce more milk, and the quality of milk itself—from pesticide residues in the feed that pass into the milk to hormones injected into the cow—raise the concern of the consumer. When milk is produced on a smaller scale, this less-intensive approach enables the plant-eating cow to enjoy her natural diet and live a healthier life, passing the benefits on to the consumer. Obviously this is much better. But what if we also provided the cow with a healthy environment and a diet free from potentially harmful chemicals? These steps are taken every day by the farmers who make up Organic Valley®.

About Organic Valley®

Organic Valley is the world's largest organic farmer-owned cooperative, with 622 farmers in seventeen states. Their stated mission is to produce the most nutritious, wholesome organic products possible. Organic Valley strives to maintain sustainability for the farmer, the promotion of cooperative principles in all phases of the farming operation, and awareness and respect for the dignity and interdependence of human, animal, plant, soil, and global life. This sounds pretty good, doesn't it?

In keeping with its mission, Organic Valley produces milk without antibiotics, BGH, or other synthetic hormones or pesticides, and its cows are fed 100% organic grains, or graze in 100% certified organic pastures. Organic Valley takes pride in having some of the *smallest* farms in America.

The typical dairy cow in America today lives only eighteen months. Cows routinely are slaughtered when their milk production wanes. By contrast, some Organic Valley Farmers have fifteen-year-old dairy cows, with the average being five years or older. Organic Valley takes an active role in animal welfare legislation and upholding the true dictates of the organic label (see Section Three: *Organic Farming*). These extra steps ensure that Organic Valley produces a nutritionally superior milk product. For more information on Organic Valley, visit: http://www.organicvalley.com/

NUTRITIONAL BENEFITS

A single 8-ounce cup of Organic Valley low-fat milk provides an impressive amount of important nutrients:

Nutrients	Organic Valley Low-fat Milk 1 cup (8 oz.)
Protein	8 grams
Calcium	30% Daily Value (DV)
Vitamin D	25% DV
Vitamin B_{12}	25% DV
Vitamin B_2	25% DV
Potassium	11% DV
Vitamin A	10% DV

NUTRITIONAL CAVEATS

Research has demonstrated that excessive saturated fat in the diet, particularly the saturated fat called *myristic acid* (see Section Three: *Fats & Oils*), increases a person's heart disease risk by raising total cholesterol and LDL (low-density lipoprotein) cholesterol levels in the body. As you can see below, a cup of whole milk has five grams of saturated fat, or 25% of the daily recommendation. To establish a healthy saturated fat intake, some individuals choose organic whole milk, while maintaining moderation with or avoiding red meat, cheese, butter, and ice cream.

Nutrients	Whole Cow's Milk 1 cup (8 oz.)	Cow's Milk—2% 1 cup (8 oz.)	Organic Valley Low-fat Milk (1%) 1 cup (8 oz.)
Calories	150	120	110
Total Fat	8 grams	4.5 grams	2.5 grams
Saturated Fat	5 grams (25% Daily Value)	3 grams (15% Daily Value)	1.5 grams (8% Daily Value)
Myristic Acid	1 gram	0.5 grams	0.25 grams

A final consideration: Not everyone digests cow's milk well. This may be evident by the inability to digest lactose (lactose intolerance) or as a reaction to specific milk proteins such as *casein* (see Section Three: *Milk Products*). Well-known medical doctors routinely advise individuals with specific health conditions, such as allergies, asthma, and chronic ear infections to eliminate milk products from their diet to see if health improves. If you choose to go milk-free for health reasons, try using soy, rice, or almond milk for at least three months before incorporating dairy back into your diet. I would like to hear from you if your condition improves (greg@hippiefood.com)

Hippie Wisdom

Cows fed organic feed and not treated with hormones such as BGH or antibiotics produce the highest quality milk in terms of your health. *Chemical residues such as pesticides accumulate in animal fats.* This makes it all the more important to choose organic animal fats.

• Choose milk and milk products from cows fed an organic diet,
• Choose organic *lowfat* dairy products when possible, and
• If you do not tolerate milk very well, look for non-dairy milk alternatives in the natural foods market including soy, almond, oat and rice milks.

Soy Milk

A friend of a friend loved to ride the Green Turtle Bus up the California coast all the way to Seattle. He was an "old hippie," accustomed to traveling light, but he never left his soymilk behind. A staple in Asian cuisine for hundreds of years, soymilk (a white liquid made from cooked soybeans blended with water) is also an indispensable food for hippies everywhere. Most soymilk on the market is sweetened and contains added salt. Some soymilk beverages are enriched with calcium and vitamin D to replicate the nutrients found in cow's milk. While hippies were making their own soymilk throughout the 1970s, commercially produced soymilk didn't hit the shelves until the early 1980s.

I highly recommend that you try soymilk if you've never tasted it before. Some find it an acquired taste. The first time I tried it, I wasn't overly impressed. But that was in 1990, and soymilk has improved significantly since then. Eden Foods® makes a great tasting soymilk which is the favorite for many health food enthusiasts.

About Eden Foods®

Eden Foods opened shop in 1968. By 1969, they were grinding their own flours and bottling their own oils and nut butters. In 1972 Eden Foods began importing traditional Japanese foods: sea vegetables, miso, teas, soy sauces, rice vinegar and more. In 1983, they discovered a soymilk processing technique pioneered at Cornell University and engineered in Japan. This technique led to their first soymilk product, *Edensoy.* It became the company's fastest selling item that year. In 1985, Eden Foods took a strong position for organic farming by producing soymilk using only *organic* soybeans (see Section Three: *Organic Farming*). Soon after, they decided to take a stand against the use and promotion of GMO foods (see Section Three: *Genetically Engineered Foods*).

Today, Eden Foods continues to keep close contact with their growers and suppliers. They conduct in-house testing of each batch of soybeans. In 1998, the *New York Times* hired a laboratory to test for GMOs in eleven soy- and corn-based foods. The only one that was tested free of any GMO foods was Edensoy soymilk. As Eden Foods has grown, they have maintained their commitment to producing the highest quality food possible. More than 200 family farms with 40,000 acres of organic farm land join in this commitment. For more information on Eden Foods, visit http://www.edenfoods.com/

Edensoy® Extra Original

Edensoy Extra Original soymilk is made from organic non-GMO soybeans, filtered water, and no refined sweeteners and is fortified with calcium, vitamin A (as beta carotene), vitamin B12, vitamin D, and vitamin E. It does not contain any artificial ingredients or use the dairy protein *casein* or any animal byproduct. The ingredients are:

> Purified water, organic soybeans, naturally malted organic corn and barley extract, calcium, kombu seaweed, Job's tears, organic barley, sea salt, vitamin E, beta carotene, vitamin D2, and vitamin B12

Job's tears is a little known grain used to add creaminess while kombu is a type of seaweed added to enhance the flavor and digestibility of the soymilk. Edensoy Extra Original soymilk is a good source of protein and very low in saturated fat content (see nutrition info below).

NUTRITIONAL BENEFITS

The potential health benefits associated with soymilk result from the ingredients in the soybean itself and the positive results which may occur for those who need to avoid dairy products (see Section Three: *Milk Products*). The soybean (see Section Three: *Soy Products*) is an excellent source of protein and has been shown to lower cholesterol and reduce heart disease risk when substituted for animal protein. In 1999 the Food and Drug Administration (FDA) approved the following label claim for products containing at least 6.25 grams of soy protein per serving: "Diets low in saturated fat and cholesterol that include 25 grams of soy protein a day may reduce the risk of heart disease."

In addition to being very low in saturated fat as compared with 2% cow's milk, Edensoy Extra Original provides more protein and a source of plant-based estrogens called *isoflavones*. These substances, particularly *genistein*, are being studied for their ability to reduce the cell growth-promoting effect of circulating estrogens made by the body which may reduce the risk of cancer. Researchers currently suggest roughly 50 milligrams of isoflavones each day for the possible prevention of cancer.

Soymilk is an excellent replacement for 2% cow's milk. It has 1/6th the saturated fat content, is protein-rich, and provides 41 milligrams of soy isoflavones per cup.

Nutrients	Cow's Milk–2% 1 cup (8 ounces)	Edensoy Extra Original 1 cup (8 ounces)
Calories	120	130
Total Fat	4.5 grams	4.5 grams
Saturated Fat	3 grams	0.5 grams
Myristic Acid	0.5 grams	0 grams
Calcium	30% Daily Value (DV)	20% Daily Value (DV)
Vitamin D	25% DV	10% DV
Protein	8 g	11 grams
Isoflavone Content	NONE	41 milligrams (20 milligrams genistein)

MEN AND PROSTATE CANCER

While the evidence is not yet conclusive, soy intake among men has been shown in a cross-national study of 42 countries to be significantly protective against prostate cancer.[16] A large study of predominantly vegetarian men found that frequent consumption (more than once a day) of soy milk was associated with a 70% reduction of the risk of prostate cancer.[17]

NUTRITIONAL CAVEATS

Since there is less vitamin D in Edensoy Extra Original than fortified cow's milk, consider other sources for vitamin D such as sunlight, fish, fish oils, eggs, fortified cereals, and supplements to meet your daily needs.

HOW TO USE

Edensoy Extra Original soymilk can be used like regular cow's milk on cereals, in cooking, baking, desserts, or smoothies. Edensoy comes in a variety of flavors, including original, vanilla, carob, and chocolate.

Hippie Wisdom

Soy milk can be a great replacement for regular cow's milk for a variety of reasons. I suggest that you try several before making up your mind. They all taste different to me. Even when I compare the original flavors, there are distinct flavor and texture differences. Some have more of a soybean taste. Some soymilks are thicker and creamier than others.

- Choose soy milk made with organic non-GMO soybeans,
- If you do not like the taste of one brand of soymilk, try another flavor or another brand, and
- If you do not tolerate soymilk very well (or like it), look for alternatives to soy and dairy in the natural foods market including almond, oat or rice milks.

Smoothie Royale

1½ cups Edensoy Extra Original
soymilk

8 medium-sized dates (pitted)

½ ounce raw or roasted almonds
(12 almonds)

1 cup frozen blueberries,
strawberries or raspberries

1 medium frozen banana (peel
before freezing)

1. Add soymilk, dates and almonds to a blender and liquefy for several minutes until smooth.

2. Cut the banana into 1" pieces.

3. Add the frozen fruit and blend until thick and creamy.

Note: When my friend and co-worker Jeffrey Magner and I were both living in the San Francisco area a few years back, we managed to concoct what we considered the "perfect" smoothie recipe. After many hours of taste testing, this is the recipe that tasted best to me. Jeffrey's original Smoothie Royale PLUS calls for three more dates! This shake tastes like a real milkshake but without all of the junk. Compare Smoothie Royale to a leading fast-food brand milkshake below. Take a close look at the list of ingredients.

Serves 2

Nutrition Analysis per Serving: 270 calories, 7 grams fat, 0.5 grams saturated fat, 3.5 grams monounsaturated fat, 2.5 grams polyunsaturated fat, 8 grams protein, 48 grams carbohydrates, 6 grams fiber, 60 milligrams sodium

Other Noteworthy Nutrients per Serving (DV = Daily Value):

Calcium	— 25% DV
Potassium	— 15% DV
Vitamin A	— 10% DV
Vitamin E	— 10% DV

Nutrients	Leading Fast-Food Brand Vanilla Shake (8-ounces)	Smoothie Royale (8-ounces)
Calories	285	270
Fat	16 grams	7 grams
Saturated Fat	11 grams (54% Daily Value)	0.5 grams
Myristic Acid	2 grams	0 grams
Fruit Servings	ZERO	3 servings

LEADING FAST-FOOD BRAND VANILLA SHAKE

Ingredients: Whole milk, sucrose, cream, nonfat milk solids, corn syrup solids, mono and diglycerides, guar gum, imitation vanilla flavor, carrageenan, cellulose gum, vitamin A palmitate. Vanilla Syrup: Corn syrup, water, vanilla, caramel color, vanilla bean fiber, pectin, citric acid, sodium benzoate (a preservative), calcium chloride, FD&C Yellow #5, and FD&C Yellow #6.

SMOOTHIE ROYALE

Ingredients: Soymilk, banana, blueberries, dates, almonds

Almond Milk

In addition to commercially-available soymilk, the natural foods move-ment has created an array of other non-dairy beverages. One simple milk alternative that people have made for years with their kitchen blenders is almond milk. And, while a home recipe for almond milk can produce a pleasant tasting beverage, it is not nearly as delicious as Almond Breeze®. A creamy and smooth almond milk found in most natural foods markets today, almond milk is growing in popularity today for both taste and health reasons. Using almond milk in cereal or in coffee is an easy way to incorporate some of the beneficial nutrients of almonds into your daily diet.

About Blue Diamond®

Founded in 1910, Blue Diamond® Growers is the world's largest tree nut processing and marketing company. Nearly 4,000 California almond growers produce more than one-third of California's almonds. The California almond crop exceeds one billion pounds annually and is the state's largest food export. For more information on Blue Diamond, visit: http://www.bluediamondgrowers.com/

Almond Breeze®

Almond Breeze is a non-dairy, milk-like beverage made from a sweet-ened mixture of puréed almonds and water. It is the best-selling almond milk on the market today. Unlike many other non-dairy beverages, it does not curdle or separate in hot beverages, making it a satisfying and healthy addition to coffee and tea. It even froths up well for lattes and cappuccinos. Almond Breeze is available in Original Almond, Vanilla, and Chocolate flavors.

INGREDIENTS (VANILLA FLAVOR):

Purified water, evaporated cane juice, almonds, tricalcium phosphate, natural vanilla flavor with other natural flavors, sea salt, potassium citrate, carrageenan, soy lecithin, d-alpha tocopherol (Vitamin E), Vitamin A palmitate, Vitamin D$_2$

NUTRITIONAL BENEFITS

Almond Breeze is ideal for anyone who cannot or does not want to drink cow's milk. It also is a great choice for those allergic to soy products or who otherwise are looking for an alternative to soy. Almond Breeze does contain soy lecithin, a fat component of the soybean, however, studies indicate that most allergic reactions are from soy proteins and not the fats in soy. Additionally, this tasty beverage contains no animal ingredients or hormones.

Almond Breeze provides some of the same benefits associated with eating a handful of almonds (see below) and does not contain cholesterol, saturated fat, nor added oils. It is low in sodium and an excellent source of vitamins A, D, and E.

Studies consistently have shown that the addition of almonds into the diet effectively lowers cholesterol. Two large studies have found that eating five servings of nuts each week (one serving equals a small handful) can lower heart disease risk by 30%–50%.[18] This is not such a surprise when one considers that almonds are a great source of several nutrients known to independently play a beneficial role in maintaining cardiovascular health: monounsaturated fats, vitamin E, folic acid, copper, magnesium, arginine, and an array of phytochemicals. In July 2003, the FDA issued the following health claim: *Eating 1 ½ ounces of most nuts, such as almonds*, as part of a diet low in saturated fat and cholesterol may reduce the risk of heart disease.*

Heart health isn't the only reason to add almonds into your diet. Preliminary research on animals has found that whole almonds inhibit colon cancer risk more effectively than wheat bran. Two of the

---

* 1½ ounces equals about one-third of a cup, or about 34 almonds.

flavonoids in almonds believed to be responsible for cancer cell suppression are *quercetin* and *kaempferol*. Most whole foods have a wide number of potentially beneficial properties, and in the case of almonds, the phytochemicals under current research hold great promise. In one study, nine different compounds isolated from almonds (excluding vitamin E), exhibited antioxidant properties.

A natural source of vitamin E (d-alpha tocopherol) is added to Almond Breeze. A single serving of original, vanilla or chocolate provides 50% of the daily value (DV). As you probably already know, vitamin E is good for you: it's the main fat-soluble antioxidant in the body. There is clinical and epidemiologic evidence to indicate that vitamin E may protect you against prostate and cervical cancers.

Nutrients	Cow's Milk – 2% 1 cup (8 ounces)	Blue Diamond Almond Breeze Vanilla (8 ounces)
Calories	120	90
Total Fat	4.5 grams	2.5 grams
Saturated Fat	3 grams	0 grams
Myristic Acid	0.5 grams	0 grams
Protein	8 grams	1 gram
Calcium	30% Daily Value (DV)	20% Daily Value (DV)
Vitamin D	25% DV	25% DV
Vitamin E	3% DV	50% DV
Phytochemicals	NONE	YES

TASTE

Almond Breeze won the 2004 Best Taste award from the prestigious American Culinary Institute, an independent, chef-based judging organization.

NUTRITIONAL CAVEATS

Almond Breeze contains only one gram of protein per serving. This needs to be a consideration for vegans (strict vegetarians) and others eating a low-protein diet. Almond Breeze Vanilla contains eight more grams of sugar (two teaspoons) per cup than Original flavor. I encourage my clients to also eat whole almonds in their diet to ensure that they are getting all of the benefits associated with nuts.

HOW TO USE

Use Almond Breeze as you would cow's milk, with coffee or tea, on cereals, in cooking, baking, desserts, or smoothies. In fact, try the Smoothie Royale recipe using Almond Breeze instead of soymilk.

Hippie Wisdom

Almond milk is a healthy non-dairy, non-soy beverage. When choosing almond milk consider:

- If you are closely watching added sugars, choose the original or plain flavor. Plain or original beverages are less sweet. When comparing the labels of products, remember that every four grams of *sugars* equals one teaspoon of sugar, and
- If you do not like the taste of one almond milk, experiment with others. Other non-dairy, non-soy beverages are oat milk and rice milk.

Yogurt

Yogurt is made by adding live active cultures, namely *Lactobacillus bulgaricus* and *Streptococcus thermophilus,* to various types of milk. The living cultures digest the milk sugar (lactose) and produce lactic acid. This fermentation process makes yogurt taste tangy and gives the milk a custard-like consistency. Because the lactose is largely broken down, individuals who are lactose-intolerant or experience problems digesting other dairy products usually are able to digest yogurt. Here in the U.S., we are steadily increasing our appetite for yogurt, eating eight times more yogurt than we did in 1960. Still, according to per capita statistics, some European countries consume ten times more yogurt per person than we do.

For ages, yogurt has been made using only milk and *living* cultures. Today, however, many supermarket brands of yogurt have changed this ancient recipe. They have added excessive refined sugars and preservatives and have PASTEURIZED the living cultures, making the cultures no longer beneficial. One yogurt company that has consistently produced a high-quality yogurt with all of the right stuff is Stonyfield Farm®.

> **DID YOU KNOW?**
>
> India's Ayurvedic writings describe the use of dairy products more than 6,000 years ago. Yogurt was most likely one of these staple foods. A common side dish served in Indian cuisine is a mixture of yogurt, chopped cucumbers, and spices (called *raita,* see recipe). It helps improve the digestibility of a meal and cools the palate when eaten with spicy foods.

About Stonyfield Farm®

Stonyfield Farm started in 1983 as a small farming school with only a few cows and today is the leading organic yogurt producer. With a commitment to providing the highest quality, best-tasting yogurt while supporting sustainable farming methods, Stonyfield Farm has become a leading advocate for organic food production in the U.S.

Stonyfield Farm organic yogurt is not your typical yogurt. Made with only 100% natural and certified organic ingredients, it contains *six* live active cultures. Other major brands typically have only three or four cultures. All milk used to produce Stonyfield yogurt comes from cows that were not treated with bovine growth hormone (see Section Three: *Hormones*). Stonyfield Farm is also the only U.S. yogurt brand with *inulin*, a natural dietary fiber shown to increase calcium absorption along with offering other health benefits. Visit www.stonyfield.com for delicious recipes and more information regarding the health benefits of Stonyfield Farm yogurt.

NUTRITIONAL BENEFITS

Stonyfield Farm lowfat yogurt is a nutritious food that provides a good source of protein as well as an array of vitamins and minerals. You can consume 30% of your daily calcium requirement in a single 6-ounce serving. It is also a great source of active cultures or "probiotics" which include: *Streptococcus thermophilus, Lactobacillus bulgaricus, Lactobacillus acidophilus, Bifidobacterium (bifidus), Lactobacillus casei,* and *Lactobacillus reuteri.* Probiotics promote digestive health. They increase immune function (as measured by specific markers) and reinforce the gut against pathogenic (disease-causing) bacteria. They inhibit disease-producing organisms like *E. coli* and *Salmonella,* and increase nutrient absorption while likely reducing colon cancer risk. Stonyfield Farm yogurt is the only brand in the U.S. to contain *L. reuteri,* a live culture that has been shown to be effective in both the prevention and treatment of bacterial and viral diarrhea.[19]

The digestive tract contains billions of bacteria, some beneficial and some harmful. Regularly eating yogurt is a good way to establish a healthy amount of beneficial bacteria in the digestive tract. Eating Stonyfield Farm yogurt during and after taking antibiotics can reduce the incidence of diarrhea and vaginal yeast infections, common side effects of taking antibiotics.

A 6-ounce serving of Stonyfield Farm yogurt contains two grams of *inulin*, a dietary fiber which occurs naturally in many fruits and vegetables. The average American consumes 2½ grams of inulin a day, 70% of which comes from wheat.[20] Inulin is a "prebiotic" that feeds the probiotics or beneficial cultures in yogurt, increasing their volume by as much as 5 to 10 times. In addition to adding creaminess to yogurt, there is evidence that inulin boosts calcium absorption by as much as 20%. Studies have confirmed the increased rate of absorption in young women and post-menopausal women who consumed eight grams of inulin each day. Preliminary studies also suggest that inulin can inhibit the development of cancer cells in the colon, protect against inflammatory conditions, stimulate immune function, and lower cholesterol and triglyceride levels. Look for further research which will reveal more potential health attributes of inulin in the next several years.

Overall, the evidence is resoundingly positive regarding the health benefits of yogurt. Stonyfield Farm produces a high-quality, organic yogurt product that is an excellent addition to a healthy diet.

NUTRITIONAL CAVEATS

Yogurt made from whole milk contains 20% of the daily saturated fat intake. In an otherwise healthy diet without an excess of red meat, butter, ice cream, and cheese, this amount is acceptable. Unlike milk, yogurt is not fortified with vitamin D. Consider other sources such as sunlight, fish, fish oils, eggs, fortified non-dairy beverages, fortified cereals, and supplements to meet your daily needs.

HOW TO USE

Yogurt can be eaten as part of a meal, as a snack, or added into a wide array of recipes, including smoothies, salad dressings, baked goods, and main dishes.

Yogurt is truly a good food. Give it a try if you haven't eaten it in a while. When buying yogurt, choose a brand made with top-notch ingredients. Look for yogurt that:
- Is made with organic milk (with no bovine growth hormone),
- Contains at least four added live cultures, and
- Does not contain additives.

Hippie Wisdom

If It Feels Good Do It! Raita

½ teaspoon toasted cumin powder

2 cups Stonyfield Farm organic lowfat plain yogurt

2 tablespoons, yellow onion or red onion, finely chopped

1 large cucumber, peeled and finely chopped

½ teaspoon salt

Dash red pepper (optional)

As previously mentioned, raita is a traditional Indian side dish that helps digestion and greatly cools the palate when eaten with any spicy food.

1. Toast cumin powder in small, dry skillet over low to medium heat for a minute or two. Do not burn.

2. In a serving dish, combine with yogurt, onion, cucumber, salt, and red pepper (optional).

3. Stir well and chill.

Serves 4

Serving Size: ¾ cup

Nutrition Analysis per Serving: 70 calories, 1 gram fat, 0.5 grams saturated fat, 5 grams protein, 11 grams carbohydrates, 2 grams fiber, 360 milligrams sodium

Other Noteworthy Nutrients per Serving (DV = Daily Value):

Calcium   — 20% DV

Potassium   — 10% DV

Soy Yogurt

As I mentioned earlier, the consumption of yogurt made from cow's milk in the U.S. has increased 800% since the 1960s. The growing popularity of soy foods in the last decade has created a wide array of soy-based products, and one of these is soy yogurt, which only recently was introduced to the market. You might choose soy yogurt instead of cow's milk yogurt if you are sensitive or allergic to *casein* and other components of cow's milk, or if you maintain a vegan diet (no animal-based foods). You might also choose soy yogurt for the potential health benefits found in soy products or simply because you like the taste. One of the best-tasting soy yogurt products on the market is produced by the WholeSoy® Company.

About WholeSoy®

The WholeSoy Company began producing soy yogurt in May of 1999. WholeSoy yogurt products were different from the other two soy yogurts on the market at the time because neither of these contained living cultures, a key health benefit associated with yogurt. Using an innovative Swedish processing method to create a smooth and good tasting soy base, WholeSoy began adding live probiotic cultures to create a healthier soy yogurt. Today, WholeSoy's cultured yogurt products are also made from non-GMO, third-party certified organic soybeans (see Section Three: *Organic Farming*) and the company supports agricultural practices aligned with making our food supply more sustainable. As an example, WholeSoy emphasizes the importance of eating "lower on the food chain," i.e., eating soybeans directly instead of using them to feed livestock as a way to increase the amount of food available to feed people. For more information on WholeSoy, visit http://www.wholesoycom.com/

WholeSoy Creamy Cultured Soy

The WholeSoy creamy cultured soy process uses live, dairy-less cultures. All of WholeSoy's cultured products today contain the following four cultures: *Streptococcus thermophilus*, *Lactobacillus bulgaricus*, *Lactobacillus acidophilus*, and *Bifidobacterium bifidus*. Organic raw cane sugar is then added to feed the live cultures and thus promote the fermentation process that gives it a tangy taste.

WholeSoy Soy Creamy Cultured Soy products are sold in 6-ounce cups in Plain, Peach, Strawberry, Raspberry, Vanilla, Lemon, Cherry, Mixed Berry, Strawberry Banana, Apricot Mango and Blueberry flavors as well as a 24-ounce Plain.

NUTRITIONAL BENEFITS

WholeSoy Creamy Cultured Soy is a tasty creamy dairy-like yogurt with all the advantages of soy and living active cultures but none of the disadvantages of its dairy counterpart—lactose, casein, whey, cholesterol or animal protein (see Section Three: *Milk Products*). The active cultures in the WholeSoy cultured products promote digestive health, increase immune function, increase nutrient absorption, and reinforce your intestinal tract against pathogenic bacteria, such as *E. coli*, *Salmonella*, *Staphylococcus*, and *Listeria*. While still preliminary, there is evidence that the beneficial bacteria found in yogurt can even lower your risk of colon cancer. WholeSoy Creamy Cultured Soy also contains 33 milligrams of isoflavones per serving (see Section Three: *Soy Products*). Isoflavones are phytoestrogens that may reduce the risk of breast and prostate cancer.

Replacing regular cow's milk yogurt with WholeSoy Plain Creamy Cultured Soy provides other nutritional benefits. WholeSoy has less than half of the total fat and none of the saturated fat found in cow's milk yogurt (see chart on page 59), and it contains comparable levels of both protein and potassium.

Nutrients	Whole Cow's Milk Yogurt 1 serving (6 oz.)	WholeSoy Plain Creamy Cultured Soy 1 serving (6 oz.)
Calories	135	150
Total Fat	7 grams	3 grams
Saturated Fat	5 grams (25% DV)	0 grams
Myristic Acid	1 gram	0 grams
Protein	7 grams	6* grams
Isoflavones	0 milligrams	33 milligrams
Fiber	0 grams**	2 grams
Calcium	30% DV	8% DV
Potassium	7% DV (260 mg)	6% DV (200 mg)

*All soy protein
**Stonyfield Farm (see food category: *Yogurt*) contains 3 grams of fiber

NUTRITIONAL CAVEATS

WholeSoy Creamy Cultured Soy contains less calcium than cow's milk yogurt, and like cow's milk yogurt, none of the WholeSoy yogurt products are fortified with vitamin D. To benefit from adequate vitamin D intake, choose good sources including: sunlight, fish, fish oils, eggs, as well as fortified non-dairy beverages, fortified cereals, and supplements.

Soy yogurt is an excellent non-dairy choice. Try a variety for taste comparisons. When buying soy yogurt, choose:
- Products made from organic, non-GMO soybeans, and
- Products with at least *four* active cultures.

Hippie Wisdom

Cottage Cheese

Cottage cheese was one of the earliest types of cheese eaten in America and has remained a popular food throughout the years for many good reasons. Unlike aged cheeses, cottage cheese requires no ripening period. It is made through a process that separates the casein protein components of non-fat milk, known as the curd, from the remaining liquid or whey. After draining off the whey, a dressing of cream, fat-free milk, and salt is then mixed with the curds to create regular cottage cheese. Other familiar

unripened cheeses on the market include ricotta, cream cheese, farmer's cheese, feta, and fresh mozzarella.

Cottage cheese is also a nutrient-dense source of animal protein and because of this, it is a favorite among the health conscious, from those trying to lose weight to the serious bodybuilder. Since cottage cheese is a dairy product, choosing quality organic milk and cream produced without the use of antibiotics, added growth hormones, or pesticides is highly recommended (see Section Three: *Organic Farming*). Remember, pesticides and other chemicals have been shown to accumulate in the fat of animals (see Section Three: *Environmental Chemicals*) so it is wise to take extra steps to minimize exposure to these environmental contaminants. One company that is committed to producing great-tasting, organic dairy products is the leading maker of organic cottage cheese. That company is Horizon Organic®.

About Horizon Organic®

More than twelve years ago, when there were very few organic products on the market, Horizon Organic began making organic yogurt. Today, with milk supplied from more than 200 organic farmer partners,

Horizon Organic is one of the nation's top certified organic food companies—producing the leading brand of certified organic milk and offering a full line of certified organic dairy products, infant formula, juices and desserts.

The best news for the consumer is that Horizon Organic produces the milk used for its organic cottage cheese without the use of antibiotics, added growth hormones, or pesticides, and their dairy cows get only certified organic feed. As part of Horizon Organic's commitment to quality, these same cows also have access to clean water, fresh air, pasture, and regular exercise. For more information on Horizon Organic, visit http://www.horizonorganic.com/

Horizon Organic Lowfat Cottage Cheese

The Horizon Organic lowfat cottage cheese process begins with Horizon Organic fat-free milk and living cultures (*Lactobacillus acidophilus* and *Bifidobacterium bifidus*). The cultures produce lactic acid which coagulates the proteins in milk. The coagulum is then cut into squares to form the curd. The mixture of curds and whey is then cooked and gently stirred. After the cooking process, the whey is drained and a lower fat dressing is added to produce lowfat cottage cheese while calcium is added to help restore that lost during the process of separating the whey. The texture of the cottage cheese is enhanced by the addition of two natural thickeners, locust bean gum and carrageenan. In addition, all Horizon Organic cottage cheese products are certified kosher.

HORIZON ORGANIC COTTAGE CHEESE INGREDIENTS

> Organic Grade A pasteurized and cultured nonfat milk, organic milk and cream, organic nonfat milk, salt, tricalcium phosphate, locust bean gum, carrageenan, microbial enzyme (non-animal, rennetless) live and active *Lactobacillus acidophilus* and *Bifidobacterium bifidus* cultures

Nutritional Benefits

One-half cup of Horizon Organic lowfat cottage cheese provides the same amount of high-quality protein (13 grams) as two ounces of cooked lean meat, poultry, or fish. Lowfat cottage cheese is a healthy, high-protein food that is quick and easy to eat as a snack or as part of a meal.

The calcium content of a serving of Horizon Organic lowfat cottage cheese is 15% of the daily recommended value. Aside from the role of calcium in osteoporosis prevention, regularly eating calcium-rich, lowfat dairy products may offer other health benefits. Studies show that adding lowfat dairy products into a healthy diet can help lower blood pressure[21] and may also lower your risk of colon cancer. [22]

As seen with yogurt, the addition of *Lactobacillus acidophilus* and *Bifidobacterium bifidus* cultures in Horizon Organic cottage cheese provides a source of beneficial bacteria to the intestine and helps deter the growth of harmful bacteria. There are numerous other benefits to having active cultures in the diet, including enhanced immune function, improved digestion, and possibly, a lowered risk of colon cancer.

Hippie Wisdom

Lowfat cottage cheese is a quick, convenient protein source that makes a great partner for fruit. Try cottage cheese with fresh, frozen or canned versions of your favorite fruit, such as pineapple, peaches, or blueberries. Choose cottage cheese that:
- Is made from organic ingredients,
- Contains live cultures, such as *Lactobacillus acidophilus* and *Bifidobacterium bifidus*, and
- Is fortified with calcium.

Butter Alternative

Butter is made from cow's milk. It has been a staple food in the human diet since the early days of agriculture thousands of years ago. In an otherwise sparse diet, butter provides much-needed fat and energy. The earliest settlers of America (from Europe) sold much of their butter supply to English creditors before setting sail on the Mayflower in 1620. Half of the pilgrims died during their first winter in New England, the loss of butter undoubtedly being a major reason for their demise.

> **DID YOU KNOW?**
>
> *Ghee* is a type of butter used in Indian cooking. It is heated (clarified) to remove lactose and other milk solids. It is solid at room temperature, but unlike butter it requires no refrigeration and does not easily spoil.

In the U.S. today, we do not have such concerns as there is definitely no shortage of calories here. We do, however, consume only one-third of the butter we did 60 years ago. Despite its one time status as "favorite spread" for toast and waffles, public concern about butter's saturated fat content and its relationship to heart disease risk had an impact on its popularity. When companies began heavily touting the health benefits of margarine during the 1960s, butter sales were already in a sharp decline. Today we know that eating hard-stick margarine is more harmful to overall health than butter (see Section Three: *Fats & Oils*), and many people have decided to switch back to the golden wonder.

About Earth Balance®

Don't forget, though, that butter is still a highly saturated fat. Research shows that, compared to other fats and oils, butter can significantly increase total cholesterol and LDL cholesterol levels.[23] As a result, health conscious consumers have been on the lookout for a suitable butter replacement— one that's made from quality oils—one that actually tastes good! Earth

Balance, a carefully crafted blend of expeller-pressed oils (soybean, palm fruit, canola seed, and olive) may be the healthiest butter replacement on the market today. Evidence from numerous human and animal studies (see below) indicates that Earth Balance is well worth a try.

EARTH BALANCE INGREDIENTS

> Expeller-pressed natural oil blend (soybean, palm fruit, canola, and olive), water, salt, natural flavor, soy protein, soy lecithin, lactic acid, and beta-carotene

Earth Balance contains no animal products, no hydrogenated oils, and no GMO products (see Section Three: *Genetically Engineered Foods*). In fact, a team of researchers from Brandeis University was granted a patent for establishing the precise blend of saturated, monounsaturated, and polyunsaturated fats in Earth Balance. The team discovered that its patented formula actually raised the "good" (HDL) cholesterol and the total cholesterol to HDL cholesterol ratio when used as part of a healthy diet. This is good news for all of us.

Over the last decade, nutrition research has confirmed that not all saturated fats are created equal. For years, palm oil has been unfairly blacklisted because of its high saturated fat content, though research consistently has found that palm oil does not adversely affect cholesterol levels and in many cases improves the cholesterol ratio.[24,25] Palm oil consists of 50% **unsaturated** fats, a class of fats that *lowers* cholesterol levels.

The addition of palm oil makes Earth Balance solid, like butter, at room temperature. But the evidence, as we just reviewed, does not implicate palm oil as raising cholesterol levels. Let's take a closer look at the different *types* of saturated fats that are at the center of the cholesterol controversy: *lauric acid, myristic acid*, and *palmitic acid*. These fats differ from one another only slightly in chemical structure (see Section Three: *Fats & Oils*). Evidence implicates myristic acid as having the most negative effect on cholesterol levels.[26] Unlike butter, palm oil contains no myristic acid. For more information on Earth Balance, visit http://www.earthbalance.net/

NUTRITIONAL BENEFITS

Studies show that butter, with a higher saturated fat and myristic acid content, raises cholesterol levels to a greater extent than any of the oils in Earth Balance. Butter fat can also be a source of harmful chemical residues including pesticides that accumulate in animal fat (see Section Three: *Environmental Chemicals*) while Earth Balance contains no animal fats.

Nutrients	Butter 1 tablespoon	Earth Balance 1 tablespoon
Calories	100	100
Total Fat	11 grams	11 grams
Saturated Fat	7 grams (35% Daily Value)	3 grams (15% Daily Value)
Myristic Acid	1.5 grams	0 grams
Trans Fat	No	No
Sodium	125 mg	120 mg

NUTRITIONAL CAVEATS

Because Earth Balance has as many calories per tablespoon as butter, it needs to be used with awareness. I like to use delicious fat sources, like almond butter or avocado, as a spread on toast or in other foods when appropriate. These whole foods offer important nutrients like magnesium and folic acid not found in Earth Balance or butter.

HOW TO USE

It is worth restating: Earth Balance tastes good. Use it in place of butter, on toast, baked potatoes, rice, pasta, vegetables, popcorn, and in recipes that call for butter.

Hippie Wisdom

Butter replacements work well for some people. It's all a matter of choice. When choosing a healthy butter replacement, find one that you really enjoy. Look for brands that:

- Are made with healthy, expeller-pressed oils,
- Contain no trans fats* (hydrogenated oils),
- Are made with no GMO ingredients, and
- Do not contain a long list of chemicals.

* Be aware: by law, a food product can contain up to 0.5 grams of trans fat *per serving* and still be labeled "trans fat-free."

Bread

Bread has been a mainstay since the earliest days of agriculture, some 10,000 years ago and remains so in most ethnic cuisines. Consider a few of the forms that bread takes: tortillas (Mexico), injera (Ethiopia), naan (India), focaccia (Italy), pita bread (Middle East), and of course, good old Wonder® Bread* (United States).

DID YOU KNOW?
In 1879 the average American ate 225 pounds of wheat flour each year. Today annual consumption is closer to 145 pounds.

Bread and other carbohydrates have been maligned by the best-selling diets in the United States, and yet, interestingly, the cultures that consume more bread than Americans are considerably *thinner.* Germans lead European countries by eating an estimated 186 pounds of bread per person each year; but unlike Americans, their bread is made mostly from whole grains.

Why Whole Grain?

First, let's distinguish whole-wheat flour from white flour. Both flours originate with the wheat berry, a seed that consists of the bran, the germ, and the endosperm. Whole-wheat flour is made by grinding the entire wheat berry into a fine powder. White flour is made from *only* the starchy endosperm—the wheat bran and the wheat germ are removed. The problem is that in the process of creating white flour, most of the beneficial nutrients are lost. These nutrients play a key role in cardiovascular health, blood sugar regulation, and cancer prevention (see Section Three: *Wheat Products*).

Another key distinction between white and whole-wheat flour—and one that is more noticeable—is the fiber that is lost when bran is removed. Bran, which helps the digestive tract maintain regularity, is found in whole-wheat flour and other whole grain flours but not in the flour that goes

---

*The Wonder® trademark is registered to the Interstate Brands Company.

into white bread. Americans spend in excess of $700 million on unnatural laxatives each year rather than choosing to eat more fiber-rich foods.

And finally, a lesser-discussed topic but still a major concern to health enthusiasts, is the widespread use and acceptance of the chemical additives in most supermarket bread today (see Section Three: *Food Additives*). These additives, designed to improve texture and increase shelf life, are considered "safe" for the most part. What this means is that there were no measurable health risks when tested. But it is worth noting that additives and preservatives in processed foods today have only been in the diet for a few decades. They are not "native" chemicals readily recognized by the body. Since we are unclear whether these chemicals contribute to serious health problems over time, a much healthier option is to choose whole grain bread with whole and simple ingredients. You can find a selection of whole grain breads, including breads made by Food for Life®, in your local natural foods market.

About Food for Life®

Forty years ago, Food for Life began baking sprouted grain and all-natural bakery products. With the mission to produce only the highest quality baked goods, Food for Life chooses the finest natural ingredients for optimum health. Today the company produces more than sixty different bread products. It continues to use its original baking techniques: no dough conditioners, additives, preservatives, artificial flavors, or artificial colorings. All ingredients used in Food for Life's bread products are natural and verified non-GMO. All organic ingredients used are third-party certified and Food for Life uses only filtered water. All products are certified kosher.

Food for Life has perfected a baking process that ensures proper moisture, texture, and flavor without compromising the nutritional value of the breads, and it is a complicated process. It begins with the sprouting of organic grains in small batches before baking them into bread. Sprouting activates enzymes that initiate the conversion of complex starches into simple sugars. The enzymes partially digest phytates (which can bind to nutrients) in the hull of the seed. The process deactivates enzyme inhibitors and other anti-nutrients and increases the utilization of protein as well as the availability of certain vitamins and minerals. For more information on Food for Life, visit http://www.food-for-life.com/

NUTRITIONAL BENEFITS

Whole-wheat contains significantly more vitamins and minerals than white flour. In a single slice of bread, whole-wheat bread has *two* times more calcium and copper, *three* times more potassium, *four* times more zinc and fiber, *five* times more manganese, *six* times more magnesium, *eight* times more vitamin B6, and *eighteen* times more vitamin E than a slice of white bread!

While U.S. adults consume almost seven servings of grain products per day, amazingly only ONE serving per day is *whole grain*.[27] Many of the nutrients missing from white bread play critical roles in carbohydrate metabolism and blood sugar regulation. White bread is missing the fiber which helps slow the absorption of dietary sugars. In addition to helping keep diabetes away, this gives us energy dispersed over a longer period of time.

Food for Life breads are also an excellent source of phytochemicals. Some of these are potent antioxidants that exert beneficial effects in the colon. Wheat bran specifically contains a complex array of chemicals, including *phytosterols*, *tocopherols* (vitamin E) and *polyphenols*, each having antioxidant and/or anti-inflammatory properties. Research has shown that the fat-soluble substances in wheat bran inhibit colon cancer in animals. Studies of individuals with colon cancer matched against other folks with no colon cancer have found that the fiber from whole grains lowers colon cancer risk.[28] So, what breads are you going to select to build and maintain a healthy digestive tract?

Food for Life® Breads

Food for Life makes six different sprouted grain breads, Ezekiel 4:9 Sprouted Grain Bread, Ezekiel 4:9 Sesame Sprouted Grain Bread,

Ezekiel 4:9 Cinnamon Raisin Sprouted Grain Bread, 7-Sprouted Grains Bread, Sprouted Whole-Wheat Bread, and Genesis 1:29 Sprouted Grain & Seed Bread. Food for Life products are often refrigerated or frozen to help extend the shelf life because they are not made with preservatives. All of the ingredients in Food for Life breads are simple, **whole-some** ingredients.

Compare the following ingredient lists, keeping in mind in this case, that "Less is more. . . ."

FOOD FOR LIFE SPROUTED WHOLE-WHEAT BREAD:

Organic sprouted wheat, filtered water, honey, molasses, fresh yeast, lecithin (from soybean), malted barley, sea salt

SUPERMARKET "WHOLE-WHEAT" BREAD:

Enriched wheat flour, water, high fructose corn syrup, whole-wheat flour, yeast, wheat bran, soybean oil, brown sugar, ethoxylated mono and diglycerides, mono and diglycerides, salt, wheat gluten, soy lecithin, calcium sulfate, potassium bromate, sodium stearoyl lactylate, calcium dioxide, calcium iodate, alpha amylase, molasses, soy flour, vinegar, datem, soy fiber, triticale, rye meal, oats, cornmeal, cracked wheat, monocalcium phosphate, flaxseed hulls, ammonium sulfate, calcium carbonate, vinegar, calcium proprionate

Hippie Wisdom

Keep white, fluffy breads in your diet to a minimum. Look for the word *whole* when reading the ingredient list of whole-wheat breads. Most bread contains white flour (often labeled as enriched wheat flour, multi-grain, or even 100% wheat flour). Choose breads that:

- Contain at least two grams of fiber per 80-calories (usually one slice),
- Are made from *only* whole grains such as whole-wheat, whole-spelt, kamut and rye,
- Contain organic ingredients,
- Do not contain additives, and
- Are made with sprouted grains.

Almond Butter

When my clients ask me to rank the healthiest nuts to add to their diet, I rate almonds at the very top. A significant body of research has revealed the many benefits of almonds, including the ability to lower cholesterol and stave off the risk of diabetes. Even a single handful of almonds provides key nutrients that can help maintain a healthy heart. No wonder almonds are the most consumed tree nut in the United States.

Spanish missionaries brought almonds to California in the mid–1700s because they thought that they would grow well in California's climate; they were right. This nut thrives in climates characterized by moist, mild winters and hot, dry summers such as those found in California, Italy, Spain, South Africa, and Australia.

One of my all-time favorite foods is almond butter. It's simply made by pressing raw or roasted almonds into a paste like peanut butter. Like most Americans, I grew up eating peanut butter and have joked that apples, bananas and celery really are "peanut-butter-delivery-systems." Many of my clients believe that almond butter, crunchy or smooth, is more delicious than peanut butter. Try an AB & J (almond butter and jelly) sandwich and see for yourself.

> ## QUOTES OF INTEREST
>
> "Those who would eat two to three almonds each day need never fear cancer."
> —Edgar Cayce, renowned psychic healer
>
> "Seven almonds a day will keep the doctor away!"
> —Ramona Ursula Lyon Dodson, a 100-year-old California girl

About Woodstock Farms®

The United Natural Foods® Company established the Woodstock Farms label in the late 1980s. The Woodstock Farms product line was developed to meet the demands of the health conscious consumer seeking quality food made with natural and organic ingredients. Woodstock Farms has established relationships with small farmers and reliable suppliers who embrace sustainable agriculture and the future of the organic movement (see Section Three: *Organic Farming*). In addition to almond butter and tahini (see food category: *Tahini)*, Woodstock Farms offers hundreds of products, many of them organic, including frozen fruits, vegetables, sugars, rice, and a variety of snack foods.

NUTRITIONAL BENEFITS

Almonds are a nutritional powerhouse containing significant amounts of protein, calcium, fiber, magnesium, folic acid, potassium, and vitamin E. Almond butter has extremely low saturated fat content and is rich in monounsaturated fats making it a heart-healthy choice (see Section Three: *Fats & Oils)*.

Studies consistently have shown that the addition of almonds into the diet effectively lowers cholesterol. In a study of 45 individuals, adding 3½ ounces of almonds—or 640 calories—into the diet every day for only four weeks significantly lowered total cholesterol and LDL cholesterol despite increasing total fat intake from 30% to 39% of calories.[29] The beneficial HDL cholesterol remained the same, thereby improving the total cholesterol to HDL ratio. Unlike low-fat, high-carbohydrate diets, adding almonds does not adversely alter insulin sensitivity in healthy adults or blood sugar levels in patients with diabetes.

Preliminary research is finding that adding almonds to the diet lessens the risk of colon cancer as well. Scientists believe that almonds may do so even more effectively than wheat bran. In addition, two flavonoids in almonds, *quercetin* and *kaempferol,* are believed to be responsible for cancer cell suppression. In related laboratory tests, two compounds in almond skins, *catechin* and *protocatechuic acid,* were found to be the most potent antioxidants of nine different compounds studied.[30] The relevance of this research is that newly identified chemicals in almonds and other whole foods are being discovered on a regular basis.

Almonds are packed with vitamin E, providing more than 35 percent of the daily value in one single handful. Interestingly, most clinical studies have been conducted using a synthetic form of vitamin E (listed on supplements as dl-alpha tocopherol) whereas food contains a complex of compounds loosely classified as vitamin E. There is an important difference between synthetic vitamin E and the eight compounds called "mixed tocopherols." The evidence is now supporting food sources of vitamin E over supplements. One particular form of vitamin E called *gamma tocopherol* is more strongly correlated to lower cancer risk than any other, and almond butter is an excellent source of gamma tocopherol. Ongoing research is investigating the ability of vitamin E to protect against an array of cancers, including cancer of the breast, cervix, prostate, and rectum.

Almonds are a good source of plant sterols, such as *beta-sitosterol*, which have been shown to alleviate symptoms of BPH (enlarged prostate), a condition afflicting the majority of men over age 50. In a study of 200 men, subjects receiving 20 milligrams of beta-sitosterol three times daily had significant improvements in symptoms and urinary flow parameters compared to men taking a placebo.[31] Two tablespoons of almond butter contain roughly 35 milligrams of beta-sitosterol.

A side-by-side comparison reveals the advantages of choosing almond butter to spread on a slice of toast instead of butter. Notice the saturated fat and myristic acid differences (see Section Three: *Fats & Oils*).

Nutrients	Butter (1 tablespoon)	Woodstock Farms Almond Butter (1 tablespoon)
Calories	100	100
Percent fat	100%	85%
Saturated Fat	7 grams (35% Daily Value)	1 gram
Myristic Acid	1.5 grams	0 grams
Magnesium	0% DV	13% DV
Phytochemicals*	NO	YES

*Remember, phytochemicals are a large class of potentially beneficial compounds found in whole plant foods.

HOW TO USE

Almond butter has a wonderful flavor and can be eaten plain, used like peanut butter in sandwiches, on bananas, apples, celery, and crackers, in smoothies and casseroles, on baked sweet potatoes, or as part of a dressing or sauce (see recipe).

Try almond butter ASAP if you've never tasted it before. It is a healthy and convenient food and the preferred nut butter for many. When buying almond butter, look for:

- A simple ingredient list that contains only almonds or almonds and salt, and
- Almond butter made from organic almonds.

Hippie Wisdom

Afterglow Almond Butter Dressing

½ cup Woodstock organic smooth almond butter

¼ teaspoon red pepper flakes

1 tablespoon Bragg Liquid Aminos® (see food category: *Soy Sauce Alternative*)

2 tablespoons nutritional yeast (see food category: *Nutritional Yeast*)

1 tablespoon + 1 teaspoon brown rice vinegar (or rice vinegar)

1 crushed garlic clove (or ½ teaspoon minced)

1 teaspoon curry powder

¾ cup vegetable broth (canned or from powder)

¼ teaspoon salt (depends on amount of sodium in broth— taste before adding)

1. Combine all ingredients in a blender.
2. Purée until smooth.
3. Chill.
4. Use on cooked vegetables or as a salad dressing. Will keep refrigerated for one week.

Serves 10

Serving Size: 2 tablespoons

Nutrition Analysis per Serving: 90 calories, 9 grams fat, 0.5 grams saturated fat, 5 grams monounsaturated fat, 1.5 grams polyunsaturated fat, 3 grams protein, 4 grams carbohydrates, 0.5 grams fiber, 200 milligrams sodium

Other Noteworthy Nutrients per Serving (DV = Daily Value):

Vitamin B1 — 65% DV
Vitamin B2 — 55% DV
Vitamin B6 — 50% DV
Vitamin B3 — 30% DV
Vitamin E — 10% DV
Magnesium — 10% DV

Vitamin B12 — 10% DV
Folate — 8% DV
Calcium — 4% DV

Cereal

More than 80 million Americans begin their day with a bowl of breakfast cereal. That makes the United States fourth in per capita cereal consumption at 160 bowls per year. Guess who eats more cereal? You're right if you guessed Ireland, England, and Australia. Behind only soft drinks and milk, breakfast cereal is the third most profitable section in the supermarket. Who would have guessed this to be possible when the Kellogg brothers, John Harvey and William Keith, started producing and selling cereal from their Battle Creek Toasted Corn Flake Company in the late 1800s? Someone else thought that there was a big future in breakfast cereal. C.W. Post created Grape Nuts® in 1897, establishing his competing business also in good old Battle Creek, Michigan, or as it is commonly called, "Cereal City."

Today cereal recipes have changed. Very few offer the quality nutrition of the cereals once made by Post and the Kellogg brothers, and many contain sugar as their first ingredient. Supermarkets today devote an entire aisle to the variety of cereals packaged with colorful labels and smiling faces. Behind the shiny cereal box facades, you will find a carefully-concocted mix of nutritionally-bankrupt refined grains and sugar, and often a vitamin and mineral supplement added to give the health-seeking consumer some incentive for buying the cereal. While a handful of nutritious cereals are still around today, most supermarket brands contain excessive amounts of sugar, partially hydrogenated oils, and questionable additives.

Fortunately, the natural foods market offers a selection of cereals, like those created by Barbara's Bakery®, made from whole grains (often organic), less refined sugars, healthier oils, and no artificial additives.

About Barbara's Bakery®

Started by 17-year old Barbara Jaffe in 1971, Barbara's Bakery has grown steadily to become a leader in the natural foods market today.

This company is committed to producing natural products made without preservatives, artificial ingredients, hydrogenated oils, or refined white sugars. Many of Barbara's Bakery products are made with organic ingredients, a step that reflects the company's support for a way of farming that is healthier for the planet, the farmers, and the consumer. Staying true to that vision, Barbara's Bakery established and runs a recycling program as well as a community service program, "Barbara's for a Brighter Future." For more information on Barbara's Bakery, visit http://www.barbarasbakery.com/

GrainShop® Cereal

Kudos to Barbara's Bakery for creating a high-fiber cereal that really tastes good. GrainShop is a medley of organic grains and quality non-GMO ingredients (see Section Three: *Genetically Engineered Foods*). Nutritionally, it's supreme, providing an impressive eight grams of fiber per 90-calorie serving. Just compare the ingredients of GrainShop with a leading high-fiber competitor, and you will see what I mean.

INGREDIENTS OF GRAINSHOP CEREAL:

> Organic wheat bran, organic whole oats, organic whole-wheat, corn bran, organic corn meal, organic dehydrated cane juice, organic barley malt extract, organic oat bran, sea salt, baking soda

INGREDIENTS OF LEADING SUPERMARKET BRAND CEREAL:

> Whole-wheat, wheat bran, sugar, high fructose corn syrup, salt, malt flavoring, vitamins and minerals, BHT

Notice that the leading brand uses two different refined sweeteners, sugar and high fructose corn syrup. All ingredients are listed in order of weight ranging from highest to lowest. Multiple types of sugar are commonly used in cereals and interspersed among ingredients so that it appears that there is more grain than sugar. Using only one type of sugar might make it the heaviest ingredient—and place it first on the list. Also, when choosing a healthy cereal, consider the quality of ingredients (whole grain, organic, non-GMO), the types of added oil (if any), the amount of fiber (aim for five grams or more per 100-calories), and the addition of preservatives (if any).

GrainShop has almost all organic ingredients, including three different whole grains (oats, wheat, and corn). The high-fiber content is a good indicator of the true content of whole-grains and wheat bran. Dehydrated cane juice is a healthier alternative to sugar and high fructose corn syrup, the sweetener found in most breakfast cereals. Barley malt extract is a slower digesting sweetener (a good thing) made from sprouted barley.

While there is no oil in GrainShop, other Barbara's Bakery cereals contain only expeller-pressed oils (see Section Three: *Fats & Oils*), and no Barbara's products contain artificial additives or preservatives. Many cereal manufacturers still use the preservative BHT (see Section Three: *Food Additives)*. Even though the Food and Drug Administration gives BHT the green light, there is some evidence in animal studies that BHT increases cancer risk and, in my opinion, should be avoided. Whole grains provide not only a wealth of beneficial nutrients, but, as one would expect, a lower risk for diseases such as cancer, diabetes, and heart disease.

Cancer

Nutrients in whole grains known to be protective against cancer include: vitamin E, folic acid, selenium, fiber, lignans, phytates, and flavonoids. In addition, whole grains provide innumerable phytochemicals. A well-designed study comparing rectal cancer patients with matched controls found that individuals consuming the most whole grains in their diet had a 30% less risk of developing rectal cancer.[32] In a similar study of colon cancer patients, control subjects eating the most whole grains had a 40% less risk of developing colon cancer.[33]

Diabetes

These nutrients in whole grains are known to be protective against diabetes: B vitamins, fiber, magnesium, zinc, chromium, and copper. Two large studies found that men and women eating the lowest cereal fiber each day (less than 3.2 grams) and the highest glycemic index foods (mostly refined carbohydrates) had *more than double the risk of developing diabetes* than those eating eight grams of cereal fiber each day and more whole grain carbohydrates.[34,35] In other words, if you are a cereal eater, keep eating high-fiber brands such as GrainShop.

Heart Disease

You've probably already guessed that there are nutrients in whole grains that are protective against heart disease. Those identified are: B vitamins, vitamin E, fiber, magnesium, potassium, manganese, copper, polyphenols, isoflavones, and, yes, those phytochemicals again. Among nearly 70,000 women in the Nurses Health Study, a five gram per day increase in cereal fiber was associated with a 37% reduced risk of developing heart disease.[36]

Hippie Wisdom

If you like to eat cereal, buying a quality brand is an exceptional way to add fiber and other nutrients into your diet. Choose cereals that contain more whole grains, less sugar, and no preservatives. Look at the ingredient list and Nutrition Facts for cereals that:

- Have five or more grams of fiber per 100-calorie serving,
- Have less than 10 grams of sugars (cereals without added fruit) or less than 20 grams (cereals with added fruit) per serving,
- Are made with organic grains, and
- Use certified non-GMO ingredients.

Smashing Bran Muffins

4 cups Barbara's GrainShop cereal

1 cup boiling water

2 Gold Circle Farms eggs, beaten

⅓ cup Earth Balance

1 cup natural cane sugar (packed) or

1 cup Sucanat® (Sucanat is a less refined cane sugar)

2 cups plain non-fat yogurt or 2 cups soymilk + 2 teaspoons lemon juice

2½ cups whole-spelt flour, sifted (see food category: *Spelt*)

2½ teaspoons baking soda

1 teaspoon salt

1½ cups raisins

1. Preheat oven to 400 degrees. Coat two muffin pans (12-count each) with a light coating of oil.

2. Pour 1 cup boiling water over the GrainShop cereal and set aside.

3. In a large bowl, cream Earth Balance and Sucanat. Add beaten eggs and yogurt (or soymilk mixture) to creamed ingredients.

4. In a separate bowl, mix spelt flour, baking soda and salt.

5. Mix with wet ingredients.

6. Fold in moistened GrainShop cereal and raisins. Do NOT over stir.

7. Fill coated muffin tins ¾ full with batter.

8. Bake 16–18 minutes at 400 degrees. Muffins are done when toothpick inserted into center of muffin tests clean.

Keep unused batter in refrigerator for up to 4 days.

Servings: 24 muffins

Serving Size: 1 muffin

Nutritional Analysis per Serving: 145 calories, 4 grams fat, 1 gram saturated fat, 1 gram monounsaturated fat, 2 grams polyunsaturated fat, 300 milligrams sodium, 28 grams total carbohydrates, 4 grams fiber, 12 grams sugar, 4 grams protein

Juice

Americans spend roughly $17 billion dollars each year on juice. Less than two-thirds of all juice produced, however, is sold as pure 100% juice. The remainder is blended in a variety of different beverages and sold as *juice drinks*. According to the Food and Drug Administration, only juices that actually consist of 100% juice can be labeled as a fruit or vegetable juice. If the beverage is diluted even slightly, the word juice must be qualified with terms such as "drink," "cocktail," or "beverage."

DID YOU KNOW?

All juices and juice drinks must indicate the percentage of juice contained in them above the Nutrition Facts label on the package.

Why Drink Juice?

Nutritional research strongly supports the relationship between fruit and vegetable consumption and lower blood pressure and reduced risk for cancer, heart disease, and other diseases. Juice contains many of the same beneficial vitamins, minerals, antioxidants, and phytochemicals found in whole fruits and vegetables. It is a convenient and delicious way to increase nutrient intake.

All Juices Are Not Equal

Quality juices are expensive to produce. As a result, many juice manufacturers have mastered the art of making juice drinks that look and taste pretty good by using small amounts of real juice and large amounts of water and refined sugars such as high fructose corn syrup. Advertising and marketing campaigns persuade consumers to buy these products. As you can see from the chart on page 81,[37] many popular "juices" are a far cry from the real thing.

Name-Brand Juice (Manufacturer)	Percent Juice
V8 Splash®	25%
Ocean Spray® Cranberry Juice Cocktail	23%
Capri Sun®	10%
Snapple®	6%
Fruitopia®	5%
Hawaiian Punch®	5%
Sunny Delight®	5%

V8 Splash is a registered trademark of Campbell Soup Company, Capri Sun is a registered trademark of Rudolf Wild GmbH & Co., Snapple is a registered trademark of the Snapple Beverage Corporation, Fruitopia is a registered trademark of the Coca-Cola Company, Hawaiian Punch is a registered trademark of Dr Pepper/Seven Up, Inc., Sunny Delight is a registered trademark of Proctor & Gamble Company

Reconstituted juices are considered 100% juice, although this must be indicated on the front of the juice label. Some manufacturers purchase flavored juice concentrate blends and simply add water to them. Juices that are freshly squeezed are healthier and more expensive, because blends are cheaper to produce than freshly squeezed juices. Even when the juice is freshly squeezed, the label is not required by law to indicate the quality of the fruit and how it was grown or processed. Most supermarket juices are often made from lower quality fruits and vegetables that contain unhealthy pesticide and herbicide residues. These unknown variables are why consumers are seeking out manufacturers who have a commitment to producing quality juices, such as R.W. Knudsen®.

About R.W. Knudsen®

The R.W. Knudsen Company is a rare breed among juice makers. Their line of quality organic juices has helped them climb to the top of the organic juice market. After 42 years in the business, Knudsen owns its own manufacturing facilities and has more control over the production process than many other juice companies. Impressively, every one of Knudsen's fruit beverages—organic or not—is made from 100% natural ingredients. All organic juices are certified organic by a third party (see Section Three: *Organic Farming*). To ensure that organic standards are being met throughout the growing season, Knudsen takes random samples from suppliers and has them analyzed for inorganic pesticides and other potential contaminants.

According to Knudsen, all juices and juice blends are carefully crafted to produce the best possible flavor. Extensive testing of raw materials for flavor, fruit sweetness, color, and acidity ensure that the quality and consistency of its juice line is maintained. Water used to make juices is well water that has been purified through carbon filtration. After production, Knudsen tastes every batch, tests it in the laboratory to verify that the appropriate standards are met, and keeps samples from *every* production run as an additional quality control measure. For more information on Knudsen juices, visit http://www.knudsenjuices.com/

I have selected two Knudsen juices to discuss in more detail, Just Concord Grape Juice and Organic Prune Juice.

Just Concord Grape Juice®

Knudsen released a new line of single-strength juices called Just Juice® in 1999. As the name says, these juices are as simple as they get. The only ingredient in Just Concord Grape Juice is the juice of ripe, organic Concord grapes.

Grape juice is an excellent source of antioxidants, potassium, magnesium, and like other plant foods, a variety of unnamed compounds that will prove to be beneficial in time.

Nutrients	Organic Just Concord Grape Juice (1 cup)
Calories	160
Potassium	250 milligrams (7% Daily Value)
Magnesium	7% DV
Calcium	8% DV
Iron	4% DV
Potent Antioxidants	YES

In the last decade, a great deal of fanfare has surrounded the research extolling the health benefits of red wine. An excellent source of the antioxidant *resveratrol*, red wine is recommended by cardiologists to reduce overall cardiovascular risk. Wine enthusiasts may not like hearing the news that 100% grape juice is an equal source of resveratrol. This antioxidant is present in the skin of grapes so only red wines—which are fermented with skins—are a good source of resveratrol. While grape juice is not fermented, the hot-press method used to extract the juice from the grape also pulls out the resveratrol present in the skin and seeds.

The benefits of resveratrol from grape juice have been demonstrated in controlled research settings. In one two-week study, healthy volunteers who drank 16 to 24 ounces [actual study used 15 ounces per 100 pounds body weight] of 100% Concord grape juice every day had a significant increase in antioxidant potential and increased resistance to LDL cholesterol oxidation (LDL oxidation is believed to increase heart disease risk). Researchers concluded that this dose of Concord grape juice has an antioxidant potential comparable to 400 IU of vitamin E.[38]

In addition to heart benefits, studies have shown that the flavonoid resveratrol promotes an anti-inflammatory response and reduces the stickiness of blood platelets, thereby reducing the risk of heart attack and stroke. Resveratrol has consistently inhibited cancer growth in laboratory experiments and based on its safety record, is considered an excellent cancer preventive candidate to use in human trials. Grape juice is a rich source of other flavonoids such as *catechin*, *epicatechin*, and *quercetin* that have been shown to inhibit breast and prostate cancer in laboratory tests using human cells.

In addition to grape, the Just Juice line includes black cherry, blueberry, cranberry, pomegranate, and organic tart cherry juices.

Organic Prune Juice®

Knudsen produces a line of *organic* juices made with at least 95% organic ingredients that are, as mentioned, independently certified to make sure that Knudsen meets all USDA organic label guidelines.

Like grape juice, prune juice is a powerhouse source of antioxidants (see below), as well as a good source of potassium, magnesium, and other beneficial nutrients. With the recent evidence that prune juice is protective against free radical damage, this juice is viewed today as more than just a tonic for maintaining regularity.

Nutrients	Organic Prune Juice (1 cup)
Calories	170
Potassium	560 milligrams (16% Daily Value)
Magnesium	10% DV
Calcium	6% DV
Iron	6% DV
Potent Antioxidants	YES

Prunes contain large amounts of phenolic compounds as measured by a technique called Oxygen Radical Absorbance Capacity (see chart below). This method, also called the ORAC test, measures the ability of a food to squelch free radicals in laboratory tests. Like the polyphenols in wine, those found in prunes are likely to be protective against chronic illnesses, such as heart disease and cancer.[39] The nutrients potassium, calcium, and magnesium found in prune juice are associated with lower blood pressure and a reduced risk of stroke.[40]

Oxygen Radical Absorbance Capacity (ORAC) of Select Foods	
Food	ORAC Score
Prunes (½ cup)	5,770
Raisins (½ cup)	2,830
Blueberries (⅔ cup)	2,400
Red grapes (1 cup)	739
Red bell pepper (⅔ cup)	710

In addition to prune juice, the other organic juices in the Knudsen organic juice line include apple, grape, grapefruit, pear, and tomato.

NUTRITIONAL CAVEATS

Unfortunately, the majority of fiber is removed whenever juice is extracted from the whole fruit or vegetable. As a result, the sugars are absorbed more quickly into the bloodstream than if the fruit were eaten whole with the fiber still intact. Too much incoming sugar can place a burden on the insulin-secreting pancreas. A major plus for Knudsen Organic Prune Juice is that it contains an impressive three grams of fiber per 8-ounce glass. This amount of fiber helps slow the absorption of fruit sugar.

While the nutrients are largely preserved in juice, so too are the calories; an 8-ounce glass of juice contains *twice* as many calories as a serving of fruit. If you are trying to lose weight, keep juice intake under control. It is easy to drink the juice of six oranges but nearly impossible to eat six oranges in a single sitting.

One other noteworthy finding relating to both red grape juice and prune juice is that the same compounds that likely protect against heart disease and cancer also inhibit iron absorption when consumed at the same time as iron-rich foods or supplements.[41] Generally, this is not a problem unless you have been diagnosed with iron deficiency anemia.

Drinking juice can be an easy way to add valuable nutrients into your diet. When buying quality juices, look for:
- Juices that are *real* juice. Look on the label for 100% juice,
- Juices made with organic ingredients, and
- Juices that provide high amounts of antioxidants, such as: prune, grape, blueberry, cherry, cranberry, tomato, and orange.

Hippie Wisdom

Soup

Soup, defined as a liquid stock containing any combination of vegetable, bean, or meat, has been a kitchen favorite for ages. Only in the last century has *canned* soup been a widely available option. Today the prepared soup market remains strong, racking up more than $17 billion annually in the United States. As people spend less and less time preparing food, canned soups will likely remain a staple grocery item.

The primary complaints against supermarket canned soup, however, are lack of flavor and/or too much sodium (salt). Until recently, there have not been any canned soups that contain lower or moderate-amounts of sodium that satisfy the palate. Fortunately, this is no longer the case. The natural foods market offers canned soup options, such as those made by Amy's Kitchen®, that contain healthier ingredients, include less sodium and taste exceptionally good.

About Amy's Kitchen®

Amy's Kitchen is a family-operated business named after the founders' daughter. The company started small in 1987 with a mission of producing truly delicious vegetarian meals made with natural and organic ingredients. Its very first product, a vegetable pot pie, was an instant success. Today the company has more than 60 different frozen meals and in 1999 introduced a grocery line of canned soups, broths, beans, chili, pasta sauces and salsas.

All of the foods produced by Amy's Kitchen are made without meat, fish, poultry, or eggs. The cheese found in some of their foods does not contain animal rennet making it acceptable for vegetarians. All of their products are either "organic" which means they contain more than 95% organic ingredients or they are "made with organic ingredients" which means that they contain 70–95% organic ingredients.

Amy's Kitchen requires all its suppliers to guarantee that ingredients used in their products are GMO-free. Where there is any question,

Amy's Kitchen makes substitutions and is sourcing from suppliers who can uphold this commitment.

Amy's Kitchen produces 14 different canned soups: Lentil, No Chicken Noodle, Minestrone, Cream of Tomato, Cream of Mushroom, Split Pea, Black Bean Vegetable, Vegetable Barley, Vegetable Broth, Organic Pasta & 3-Bean Soup, Lentil Vegetable, Organic Chunky Tomato Bisque, Alphabet Soup, and Butternut Squash Soup. Give these soups a try—you'll be impressed. For more information on Amy's Kitchen, visit http://www.amyskitchen.com/

NUTRITIONAL BENEFITS

As discussed, most supermarket soups are high in sodium and/or low in flavor. Interestingly, when you compare just the Nutrition Facts information of Amy's Cream of Mushroom with that of the leading supermarket brand cream of mushroom soup, it can be difficult to distinguish the healthier choice.

Nutrients	Leading Supermarket Brand Cream of Mushroom (1 cup serving)	¾ cup of Amy's Organic Cream of Mushroom + ¼ cup Almond Breeze Original (1 cup serving)
Calories	95	165
Total Fat	7 grams	9 grams
Saturated Fat	1.5 grams	2 grams
Sodium	810 milligrams	630 milligrams

Aside from the sodium content, they look very similar, and in some cases, the supermarket brand looks like it has the edge. But there's always more to the story. Sometimes the evidence that a product is healthier resides in the list of ingredients. Even though science is unable to easily quantify these differences, a quality soup can only be created from quality ingredients. Contrast the list of ingredients in Amy's Kitchen Cream of Mushroom with the supermarket brand mushroom soup that follows:

AMY'S KITCHEN CREAM OF MUSHROOM INGREDIENTS

Filtered water, organic mushrooms, organic onions, organic wheat flour, organic high-oleic safflower oil, organic leeks, organic grade AA butter, organic cream, sea salt, organic garlic, spices

LEADING SUPERMARKET BRAND CREAM OF MUSHROOM INGREDIENTS

Water, mushrooms, vegetable oil (corn, cottonseed, canola and/or soybean), modified food starch, wheat flour, cream, contains less than 2% of the following: salt, dried whey, MSG, soy protein concentrate, dried dairy blend, (whey, calcium caseinate), yeast extract, spice extract, dehydrated garlic

Ingredients	Leading Supermarket Brand Cream of Mushroom	Amy's Kitchen Cream of Mushroom
Organic	0 %	99%
Type of Oil	Inexpensive and less healthy corn, cottonseed, canola and/or soybean	Organic high-oleic* safflower oil
Butter/Cream	Non-organic cream	Organic butter, organic cream
Monosodium Glutamate (MSG)	Yes	No

* High-oleic safflower oil is a variety that contains more monounsaturated fats and fewer poly-unsaturated fats than regular safflower oil, making it a healthier oil (see Section Three: *Fats & Oils*).

Amy's Kitchen makes five different soups containing beans that are all an excellent source of fiber. In addition, beans provide folate, magnesium, and other phytochemicals that are lacking in the diet of most Americans and deficiencies of which can lead to heart disease, diabetes, cancer, and other health problems.

Amy's Kitchen Soup	Fiber (per cup)
Lentil	9 grams
Lentil Vegetable	9 grams
Black Bean Vegetable	5 grams
Split Pea	4 grams
Organic Pasta & 3-Bean	4 grams

Canned soup is a convenient food that can be really healthy if made with high-quality ingredients. Choose soups that:
- Contain NO preservatives,
- Are made with organic ingredients, and
- Contain less than 650 milligrams of sodium per one cup serving.

Hippie Wisdom

Crackers

With simple ingredients and a long shelf-life, the cracker is a favorite of manufacturers and consumers alike. While originally made with whole grains, the wholesome cracker unfortunately has degenerated into a highly-processed, unhealthy snack food. Sylvester Graham, the inventor of the wheat-based graham cracker in 1829, would be disappointed by the refined crackers that fill the supermarket shelves today. Until recently, the only nutritional options in stores were European-style crackers such as Ry Krisp® and Wasa®, which although nutrient dense, do not provide the taste and texture that many Americans desire. Fortunately, there are companies, such as Kashi®, who are committed to producing crackers that are both wholesome and delicious-tasting.

About Kashi®

In 1984 the Kashi Company was founded on the belief that everyone has the power to make healthful changes. The first product the company launched twenty years ago was Kashi—Seven Whole Grains and Sesame Breakfast Pilaf. As Kashi has grown, it has maintained its commitment to producing minimally-processed natural foods that are free of highly-refined sugars, unnecessary additives, and preservatives. Today Kashi's product line includes a variety of cereals, energy bars, waffles, crackers, and high-protein shakes.

The name Kashi was chosen as a combination of the words "kashruth," or kosher, and "Kushi," the last name of the founders of Macrobiotics*, Michio and Aveline Kushi. It was later that the founders discovered that Kashi means porridge in Russian, pure food in Hebrew, energy food in Japanese, and happy food in Chinese.

One of the ways that Kashi ensures the quality of its foods is through the Veri-Pure pesticide residue testing program. To qualify for

---

* Macrobiotics is a whole foods way of eating and living

the Veri-Pure seal of approval, products must test negative within 0.1 parts per million for the presence of more than 100 synthetic agricultural chemicals. While this designation is not associated with the organic certification process, it does provide the consumer with the assurance that the tested products are free from specific synthetic chemicals. Look for the Veri-Pure seal printed on select Kashi products. For more information on Kashi, visit http://www.kashi.com/

TLC® Crackers

In 2002, Kashi® began producing their TLC (stands for 'Tasty Little Crackers') in four different flavors: Original 7-Grain, Honey Sesame, Natural Ranch, and Cheese TLC Country Cheddar. The crackers are made from Kashi's combination of Seven Whole Grains and Sesame and flour, cracked whole-wheat berries, and toasted sesame seeds.

NUTRITIONAL BENEFITS

TLC crackers contain no hydrogenated oils, no saturated fat, no highly-refined sweeteners, no artificial ingredients, and only about 200 milligrams of sodium per serving. Compare Original 7-Grain TLC ingredients with a leading supermarket brand.

ORIGINAL 7-GRAIN TLC

Unbleached wheat flour, Kashi Seven Whole Grains & Sesame Flour (oats, hard red winter wheat, rye, long grain brown rice, triticale, barley, buckwheat, sesame seeds), expeller-pressed sunflower oil, evaporated cane juice, toasted whole-wheat, toasted sesame seeds, wheat bran, contains 2% or less of brown rice syrup, stone ground whole-wheat flour, sea salt, malt extract, yellow corn meal, millet, onion powder, horseradish powder, rice flour, malted barley flour, natural leavenings (potassium bicarbonate, sodium acid pyrophosphate, monocalcium phosphate), whey

LEADING SUPERMARKET CRACKER BRAND

Enriched white flour, partially hydrogenated soybean oil, defatted wheat germ, sugar, corn starch, high fructose corn syrup, salt, corn syrup, malt syrup, leavening, vegetable colors, malted barley flour

Original 7-Grain TLC includes a variety of grains including seven different *whole* grains. The fiber content (see comparison below) is a good indicator of the presence of whole grains in the cracker. The oil in TLC crackers is expeller-pressed sunflower oil, a much healthier option than hydrogenated oil (see Section Three: *Fats & Oils*). Dehydrated cane juice is used instead of high fructose corn syrup and more refined sugars found in other crackers. No Kashi product contains artificial additives or preservatives.

Many cracker manufacturers still use BHT, a preservative used to increase the shelf life of crackers. Even though the Food and Drug Administration gives BHT the green light (see Section Three: *Food Additives*), there is evidence in animal studies that BHT increases cancer risk and, in my opinion, it should be avoided.

A key nutritional advantage of TLC, evident from the Nutrition Facts information below, is the fat difference. The higher fat content of the leading supermarket brand is not the problem; it's the *type* of fat. A single serving provides 1 gram of saturated fat plus another 2 or so grams of unhealthy trans fats (see Section Three: *Fats & Oils*). Overall, Kashi TLC delivers great taste and real nutritional value.

Nutrients	Leading Supermarket Brand 16 crackers	Kashi Original 7-Grain TLC 15 crackers
Calories	150	130
Total Fat	6 grams	3 grams
Saturated Fats	1 gram	0 grams
Trans fats	YES	NO
Fiber	< 1 gram	2 grams
Sodium	270 milligrams	200 milligrams

You'll realize with some trial and error that there are NOT many delicious and healthy crackers on the market today. Try several brands to find one that you really like. When buying crackers look for those that:
- Contain whole grains,
- Contain at least two grams of fiber per serving,
- Do not use hydrogenated oils,
- Are preservative-free, and
- Contain organic ingredients.

Hippie Wisdom

Flashback Salmon Patties

15-ounce can wild Alaskan salmon (most supermarket brands)

1 Gold Circle Farms egg

2 tablespoons oil: Extra-light olive oil or Spectrum® high-oleic sunflower oil

½ teaspoon salt

1 tablespoon lemon juice

2 tablespoons onion (finely chopped)

⅓ cup whole-wheat flour or whole-spelt flour (see food category: *Spelt*)

¼ teaspoon pepper

½ cup Kashi TLC Original 7-Grain Crackers, crumbled

1. Drain salmon, reserving liquid. Set aside.
2. In a bowl mix salmon, egg, oil, salt, lemon juice, onion, flour, pepper and ¼ cup cracker crumbs. Add liquid back, as needed, to help mixture hold together.
3. Refrigerate mixture until chilled.
4. Shape into three croquettes. Roll in remaining cracker crumbs. Place on lightly greased baking sheet. Bake at 400 degrees for 30 minutes.

Serves 3

Nutrition Analysis per Serving: 420 calories, 22 grams fat, 4 grams saturated fat, 7.5 grams monounsaturated fat, 1 gram polyunsaturated fat, 33 grams protein, 21 grams carbohydrates, 3 grams fiber, 790 milligrams sodium

Other Noteworthy Nutrients per Serving (DV = Daily Value):

Omega 3s (DHA) — 1,140 milligrams
Omega 3s (EPA) — 110 milligrams
Selenium — 90% DV
Calcium — 30% DV
Vitamin E — 20%
Magnesium — 20% DV
Potassium — 15% DV
Iron — 15% DV

Crackers

Tortillas

The flatbread that the Aztecs ate for thousands of years became known as "tortillas" after Spanish conquerors landed upon the shores of the Americas in 1521. Tortillas were traditionally made from corn that had been dried, soaked in a lime solution to remove the kernels, and ground into a dough mixture called *masa*. The masa was then spread onto a griddle and cooked. In the 18th century, inhabitants of Central America migrated to the southwest regions of the United States. Wheat grew abundantly in this part of the country and quickly replaced corn as the "daily bread." The wheat tortilla became a staple food for these people and remains an integral part of Southwestern cooking today. There are many different ways the tortilla can be used in a meal, including burritos (tortilla wrapped around filling), enchiladas (tortilla wrapped around filling and then baked), tacos (filling inside a baked/fried tortilla), and quesadillas (filling folded in tortilla and toasted or fried).

> **DID YOU KNOW?**
>
> The traditional method of soaking corn tortillas in lime (calcium oxide) increases the calcium content by more than 300% and increases the available iron by 70%!

Unfortunately, 99% of wheat tortillas served in the U.S. today are made from white flour (see Section Three: *Wheat Products*). Another example of a staple food that was once nutrient-rich, the tortilla has been stripped of many healthy ingredients, and contains added dough conditioners and preservatives for the convenience of texture and longer shelf life. These additives are *not* good nutrition and, thankfully, there are healthier choices to be made. One company, Alvarado Street Bakery®, makes a delicious sprouted-grain tortilla that can be found in most natural foods markets.

About Alvarado Street Bakery®

Alvarado Street Bakery has its roots in the hippie era, having played an important role in the "Food for People, Not for Profit" movement in the

San Francisco Bay Area. Today Alvarado Street Bakery produces 30 different organic baked goods in their Northern California bakery. The company upholds its ideals of running a cooperatively-owned business while delivering the finest-quality baked goods possible (see Section Three: *Organic Farming*). One of its policies is to use whole grain and organic ingredients whenever possible and, by doing so, it actively supports the sustainable agricultural practices of its suppliers.

Alvarado Street Bakery uses no ingredient (including soy-based lecithin and corn) that has been genetically altered (see Section Three: *Genetically Engineered Foods*). In addition to being non-GMO, most of the ingredients in its products are organic (see list of ingredients), and *none* of its products contain dough conditioners, bromides, or any chemical preservatives or additives of any kind. For more information on Alvarado Street Bakery, visit http://www.alvaradostreetbakery.com/

What are Sprouted Wheat Tortillas?

Sprouted grains have been used to make breads since biblical times. Research shows that flour made from sprouted grains is easier to digest than regular flour. The sprouting process activates enzymes that digest starches into simpler sugars, inactivates *anti-nutrients* that protect the seed from predators, and actually "pre-digests" other components of the seed. After Alvarado Street Bakery sprouts organically grown wheat berries, it creates dough by adding organic whole-wheat flour, unrefined sunflower oil, sea salt, and water. The mixture is then shaped and baked slowly.

NUTRITIONAL BENEFITS

There are very good reasons to choose whole grain tortillas instead of regular supermarket tortillas. The real nutritional benefits of whole-wheat versus white flour often are understated (see Section Three: *Wheat Products*). The specific nutrients found in whole grains reduce the risk of developing disease, including diabetes, cancer, and heart disease.

Alvarado Street Bakery Sprouted Wheat Tortillas do not contain any hydrogenated oils or preservatives. Compare the ingredient lists of Alvarado Street Bakery Sprouted Wheat Tortillas with a leading supermarket tortilla brand:

ALVARADO STREET BAKERY SPROUTED WHEAT TORTILLA:

Organically-grown sprouted wheat berries, organically grown whole-wheat flour, water, unrefined sunflower oil, sea salt, aluminum-free baking powder

LEADING SUPERMARKET FLOUR TORTILLA BRAND:

Enriched bleached wheat flour, water, partially hydrogenated soybean and/or cottonseed oil, salt, baking soda, sodium aluminum sulfate, corn starch, monocalcium phosphate and/or sodium acid pyrophosphate, calcium sulfate, calcium propionate (preservative), sorbic acid (preservative), potassium sorbate (preservative), fumaric acid (dough conditioner), sodium metabisulfite (dough conditioner)

The list of ingredients can help you determine if the product is made from simple and wholesome ingredients or refined ingredients and preservatives. Aside from the list of ingredients that are difficult to pronounce, a significant difference can be found on the nutrition label (see page 97). Look at the low fiber content of the refined tortilla. Fiber content is typically a good indicator of how much whole grain is actually in a food. Unfortunately, the Nutrition Facts information does not disclose the differences in phytochemical or trace nutrient content. As I touched upon earlier, the complexity of these compounds and how they interact in the body may make the difference between good health and poor health.

Nutrients	Supermarket Tortilla	Alvarado Street Bakery Sprouted Wheat Tortilla Burrito Size
Calories	140	170
Fat	2.5 grams	3.5 grams
Saturated + Trans Fat	1.5 grams	0 grams
Fiber	1 gram	6 grams (30% Daily Value)
Beneficial Phytochemicals	Low	Significant

Whole grain tortillas make fast-food, such as burritos, much healthier. Only a few companies make really good whole grain sprouted tortillas. You are unlikely to find these foods in a regular supermarket, so go to a natural foods market and look for tortillas that are:

Hippie Wisdom

- Made with whole grains,
- Made without hydrogenated oils,
- Preservative-free,
- Made with sprouted grains, and
- Made with organic grains and non-GMO ingredients whenever possible.

Bellbottom Burritos

1 teaspoon extra-virgin olive oil

1 teaspoon ground cumin

½ medium yellow onion, chopped

½ of a medium green, yellow or red bell pepper, remove seeds and chop

½ teaspoon garlic powder

15-ounce can Eden Foods® Organic Black Beans

2 tomatoes, diced or cut into wedges

⅛ teaspoon salt*

1 cup shredded green leaf, red leaf, or romaine lettuce

1 cup salsa

2 Alvarado Street Bakery whole-wheat tortillas

1. Heat olive oil on medium heat and add cumin. Do not burn.

2. Cook gently for approximately 1 minute, and then add onion, bell pepper, and garlic powder. Cook until onions begin to soften.

3. Add black beans and chopped tomatoes. Cook for approximately 3–4 minutes, stirring to avoid burning.

4. Heat a tortilla in a large, ungreased skillet until it is warm and soft.

5. Spread half of the sauté mixture on the tortilla and top with lettuce and salsa. Fold and enjoy.

* Depends on the type of canned beans used. A higher-sodium brand requires less added salt. Taste prior to adding salt.

Serves 2

Nutrition Analysis per Serving: 400 calories, 4 grams fat, 1.5 grams saturated fat, 7.5 grams monounsaturated fat, 1 gram polyunsaturated fat, 22 grams protein, 77 grams carbohydrates, 23 grams fiber, 550 milligrams sodium

Other Noteworthy Nutrients per Serving (DV = Daily Value):

Vitamin C	— 60% DV	Iron	— 30% DV
Vitamin A	— 35% DV	Folate	— 25% DV
Potassium	— 30% DV	Magnesium	— 25% DV

Cheese Alternative

Cheese is described by author Clifton Fadiman as "Milk's leap toward immortality", and cheese-loving folks give credence to this idea. They confess that cheese is very challenging to eat *moderately*. I can understand why: variety, taste, satisfaction, and versatility. Cheese has it all. Each variety offers its own delicate blend of fat, flavor, and texture. It can be served hot or cold, with crackers, fruit or nuts, and can even be eaten straight from the package. Cheese has a powerful appeal.

> **DID YOU KNOW?**
>
> Americans consume nearly 30 pounds of cheese per person every year, a figure that has doubled in the last twenty-five years. Our ancestors considered cheese a luxury food item. Only a century ago, they ate less than an ounce per week (size of a golf ball) on average. That translates into just over three pounds a year.

You likely have a favorite cheese (or two) that catches your fancy if you eat a typical diet. When cornered, you even may say that your cheese snacking is an addiction. While cheese is perfectly designed for sustenance in cold climates (I once read an article about Finnish lumberjacks who ate blocks of cheese to fuel their 8,000-calorie-a-day needs), cheese does not fit very well in a healthy way into the diet of the person sitting behind a computer all day. In a largely sedentary culture, excessive cheese intake is a real nutritional concern. The strikes against cheese are:

- **Calories.** A single slice of hard cheese or one ounce delivers 100 calories. A quick snack of cheese and crackers can easily amount to 500 calories or 25% of the daily requirement.
- **High saturated fat content.** A single slice of hard cheese provides 25% of the daily requirement.
- **High animal fat content.** Ingesting animal fats in the diet is the primary source of environmental contaminants. High-fat cheeses are of greater concern if they are not organic because of these chemicals.

- **Dairy proteins.** Even though cheese is better tolerated than many other dairy products, it still can be an allergenic food. If you have certain health conditions, consider dairy proteins as a potential source of your problem (see Section Three: *Milk Products).*

Attempts to create healthier low-fat cheeses have failed miserably. True cheese connoisseurs say that low-fat or fat-free cheeses closely resemble the taste and texture of a rubber band, and these cheeses don't even melt! The food industry is trying to develop a variety of healthier cheese substitutes that actually *resemble* cheese. In fact, I know of a healthier cheese alternative made by Galaxy Foods® that does melt well and provides the desired cheesy texture when added to foods.

About Galaxy Foods®

Galaxy Foods started in 1972 when founder Angelo Morini invented a new way to make a cheese product free of saturated fat, cholesterol, and the milk sugar, lactose. Today, his company has become the provider of the most complete line of healthy dairy alternatives in the world. A division of Galaxy Foods called Soyco Foods® makes a dairy-free vegan cheese alternative as well as lactose-free cheese alternatives from soybeans and rice.

- **Dairy-free (vegan):** does *not* contain the milk protein casein (which gives cheese melting properties) or any other animal products
- **Lactose-free:** contains the milk protein casein but no animal fats or cholesterol

These cheese alternatives come in a wide variety of forms, including: sliced cheese, chunk cheese, shredded cheese, grated parmesan, sour cream, and cream cheese. All cheese products in the Soyco cheese line are lactose-free foods made with 100% natural ingredients. They contain no animal fats or cholesterol, and no artificial flavorings or colorings.

Rice Shreds® Mozzarella Flavor

One Soyco product is Rice Shreds, a mozzarella and cheddar flavored cheese alternative made with the following ingredients:

> Rice beverage (filtered water, organic brown rice, maltodextrin/rice
> protein), casein, rice bran oil, rice flour, tapioca flour, sodium phosphate,
> tricalcium and potassium phosphates (a source of calcium, potassium,
> and phosphorus naturally present in cheese), sea salt, natural flavors,
> citric & lactic acids, carrageenan (a sea plant fiber), vitamin E, vitamin A
> palmitate, vitamin B_2

Rice Shreds is completely soy-free. Like most lactose-free cheese
products on the market today, it contains a protein called casein derived
from cow's milk. This protein gives Rice Shreds the melting characteristics of regular cheese. Try using Rice Shreds mozzarella if you are looking
for a healthier alternative to regular cheese. For more information about
Rice Shreds, visit http://www.galaxyfoods.com/soyco.html/

NUTRITIONAL BENEFITS

Rice Shreds contains a whopping 30% of the daily value of calcium in a
single ounce. It also provides 15% of the daily value of both vitamin A and
vitamin E. The real nutritional benefits of Rice Shreds mozzarella cheese,
however, result from displacing regular full-fat cheese. Compare a single
serving of Rice Shreds with an ounce of regular mozzarella cheese.

Nutrients	Regular Mozzarella (1 ounce)	Soyco Foods Rice Shreds Mozzarella (1 ounce)
Calories	110	60
Total Fat	9 grams	3 grams
Saturated Fat	6 grams (25% Daily Value)	0.5 grams
Myristic Acid	1 gram	0 grams
Sodium	180 milligrams	340 milligrams
Protein	7 grams	6 grams
Calcium	20% DV	30% DV

There are vast differences in calorie and fat content in even a single ounce serving. Imagine the effect of eating multiple servings in a single sitting. A couple of pieces of pizza or a serving of lasagna would raise the mozzarella content to at least three ounces. This amount of mozzarella cheese comprises a full 75% of a person's daily saturated fat requirement! Remember, saturated fat raises our cholesterol levels, and, for many of us, regularly consuming full-fat cheese can make maintaining a healthy body weight much more difficult.

NUTRITIONAL CAVEATS

Rice Shreds contains the protein casein, an allergen for some individuals, and it contains more sodium per ounce than regular mozzarella cheese.

HOW TO USE

While dairy cheese is difficult to replicate, Rice Shreds mozzarella is tasty, melts well, and can be used in any recipe that uses ordinary mozzarella. I personally prefer Rice Shreds melted. I like the cheesy texture it gives to my recipes. Try it on pizza, in burritos, lasagna, and bean dishes (see recipe that follows).

Hippie Wisdom

There are some surprisingly good cheese alternatives on the market today. Be willing to experiment with several brands to find one that you like. Look for those that:
- Do not contain a long list of artificial ingredients,
- Are fortified with calcium and other nutrients,
- Contain casein if you want the cheese to melt, but
- Do not contain casein if you want to avoid all dairy products.

Power to the Pintos

1 tablespoon extra-virgin olive oil

½ teaspoon ground cumin

½ medium onion, diced (½ cup)

½ green pepper, diced (½ cup)

15-ounce can Eden Foods® Organic pinto beans

½ teaspoon salt* + ⅛ teaspoon salt

½ cup Rice Shreds mozzarella

1. Heat olive oil over medium-high heat in large skillet. Add cumin and let cook for 1 minute.
2. Add onions and green pepper and sauté for 2–3 minutes.
3. Add pinto beans and cook for 5 minutes, or until thoroughly heated.
4. Remove from heat.
5. Add Rice Shreds and stir.
6. Serve.

*Important sodium note: Do not add salt before tasting if you are using regular (higher-sodium) canned beans.

Modify this recipe by:
- Adding 3–4 chopped mushrooms with onions and green pepper and/or
- Adding ¼ cup of nutritional yeast (see food category: *Nutritional Yeast*) while cooking pinto beans

Serves 3

Nutrition Analysis per Serving: 140 calories, 2 grams fat, 0.25 grams saturated fat, 1 gram monounsaturated fat, 0.5 grams polyunsaturated fat, 8 grams protein, 18 grams carbohydrates, 7 grams fiber, 640 milligrams sodium

Other Noteworthy Nutrients per Serving (DV = Daily Value):

Vitamin C	— 30% DV	Selenium	— 15% DV
Folate	— 20% DV	Potassium	— 15% DV
Iron	— 20% DV	Magnesium	— 10% DV
Calcium	— 20% DV		

Cheese Alternative

Beans

How many Americans do you think eat more than two of the dozens of bean varieties available in a natural foods store? Aside from the occasional pork and beans served at picnics and county fairs, my own private survey among clients tells me that not many are bean eaters. Our recent ancestors depended on lima beans, black-eyed peas, and other easily-grown legumes to help meet their food needs. Studies, however, show that when people's standard of living increases, they shift away from eating beans and towards more animal-based foods. This definitely has been the case in the U.S. as we've become more affluent. The little old bean is unable to compete for our attention with the many exciting dishes centered around beef, chicken, and fish, especially when packaged as convenience foods.

Beans are a primary food among most of the world's inhabitants, including the people living in Africa, the Middle East, India, Mexico, and Mediterranean countries. Most Americans consume an average of only seven pounds of beans each year while Americans of Mexican descent average thirty-four pounds. This is of benefit for them because adding more beans into the diet is one of the easiest ways to improve overall health. Research shows that bean intake can help lower the risk of heart disease, cancer, and diabetes, and even weight control is made easier by eating more fiber-rich legumes.

> **DID YOU KNOW?**
>
> Beans contain complex sugars called *oligosaccharides* that are difficult to digest and are the source of excess gas. Three ways to reduce gas problems are:
> 1) Rinse beans prior to and during cooking (primarily dried beans)
> 2) Try adding a few drops of Beano®, a commercial product that contains the right enzymes to reduce gas. Follow directions.
> 3) Add one teaspoon of baking soda or a pinch of the sea vegetable kombu to beans while cooking.

Dried Beans vs. Canned Beans

Once harvested, you can store dried beans for a long time. In fact, shelf-life is the primary reason that beans are a staple food in many developing countries. (Relying on dried beans is also a good way to reduce packaging waste.) One of the obstacles of relying on dried beans, however, is the preparation time involved. First they must be soaked overnight in water. Then, after rinsing them thoroughly, the beans still need several hours of cooking before they are soft enough to eat. Canned beans, on the other hand, offer incredible convenience *and* a long shelf-life. Beware, though, of the sodium content found in most supermarket brand canned beans. Instead, select Eden Foods® canned, organically grown beans, a line of beans produced without any added salt.

About Eden Foods®

Eden Foods started in 1968. By 1969, the company was grinding its own flours and bottling its own oils and nut butters. By 1991, Eden Foods had located a cannery to produce canned, organically grown beans in accordance with company ideals. Initially, cannery experts told Eden Foods that it needed to add chemical preservatives to its soaked beans prior to cooking them. The idea was that the preservatives would prevent the beans from falling apart. Committed to keeping its product pure and natural, the clever folks at Eden developed a simple method of adding only water and kombu* to their beans. They proved that this simple method worked very well. Eden also discovered that the higher the mineral content of the soil in which the organic beans were grown, the more likely the beans would hold together, even better than ordinary supermarket beans. Shortly after introducing them to market, Eden's canned beans quickly became the company's fastest-growing food product, and by 1994 Eden Foods acquired its own canning facility in Indiana.

As Eden Foods has grown, the company has maintained its commitment to producing the highest-quality food possible. More than 200 family farms with 40,000 acres of organic farm land supply this excellent company. For more information on Eden Organic canned beans, visit http://www.edenfoods.com/

---

*Kombu is a type of red seaweed that is used for flavor. It is also commonly added while cooking beans as a way to improve their overall digestibility.

Eden® Organic Black Beans

Eden grows its organic black beans in nutrient-rich soil free from pesticides, herbicides, and chemical fertilizers. The beans are then soaked overnight and cooked at the company's own certified organic and kosher cannery. No salt is added during or after cooking.

Today Eden remains the only brand in the natural foods market that offers a line of canned beans (twelve different types) without any added salt. The ingredients of Eden Organic Black Beans are: organic black turtle beans, water, and kombu seaweed.

NUTRITIONAL BENEFITS

Plainly stated, beans are loaded with beneficial nutrients. They are a good source of protein, low in fat, and provide a full array of trace nutrients. In addition, beans are satisfyingly filling, especially when you consider their low calorie count. A single cup of black beans—which is only 220 calories—contains 70% of daily fiber needs, 35% of the daily value (DV) of folate*, 25% DV of iron, 25% DV of magnesium, and 20% DV of potassium. I highly recommend that you incorporate them into your diet.

Heart Disease

Many Americans are deficient in the same key nutrients found so abundantly in beans, such as fiber, magnesium, folate, and potassium. Each of these nutrients plays an important role in maintaining a healthy cardiovascular system. One 19-year study involving 9,600 men and women found measurable health benefits for regular bean eaters. Those who ate beans four or more times per week had a 22% lower risk of developing heart disease than those who ate beans less than once a week.[42] While it is difficult to pinpoint the reason for the heart benefits of beans, there

---

* Pregnant women, take notice: Beans are a superb food for you. In addition to being an excellent source of folate (proven to reduce the risk of neural tube birth defects), the fiber and magnesium in beans help your body regulate blood sugar and prevent gestational diabetes.

are many plausible explanations. For just one example, when added to the diet, folate has been shown to lower plasma levels of a compound called *homocysteine*, currently theorized to be a marker for heart disease.

Consider this: the Food and Drug Administration (FDA) has approved the following label: *"Three grams of soluble fiber in a diet low in saturated fat and cholesterol may reduce the risk of heart disease."* A single cup of Eden Organic Black Beans contains 2.5 grams of soluble fiber.

Cancer

The skins of black beans contain measurable antioxidants called *flavonoids* also found in numerous fruits and vegetables.[43] Researchers believe that flavonoids help prevent cancer. Evidence in animals shows that black beans can reduce colon cancer incidence significantly. The high-fiber content of beans helps speed the passage of waste products through the digestive tract, a factor that reduces the exposure of toxins to colon cells. Researchers also attribute the lower cancer risk to the role that beans play in controlling appetite and helping us eat fewer calories (less body fat means less risk for colon cancer).

A single serving of beans provides 35% of the daily requirement for folate. In addition to having heart-health benefits, folate is a cancer preventative. It is estimated that 10% of Americans are folate-deficient and that deficiency significantly increases the prevalence of faulty DNA synthesis. In other words, inadequate folate intake causes your body to substitute the wrong DNA base pair for the desired DNA base pair (which requires the presence of folate) during DNA synthesis. This substitution causes chromosomal breaks. Researchers theorize that this very mechanism is one of the primary causes of colon cancer.[44]

Diabetes

Beans are carbohydrate-rich foods, and some pundits have blacklisted them from many popular high-protein diets because carbohydrates are said to have a deleterious effect on blood sugar and insulin levels. This is unfortunate. Let's take a look at the facts according to the *Glycemic Index* (GI), a measure developed by researchers to assess how quickly carbohydrates are converted into glucose in the bloodstream (see chart below). Using this measure, we see that carbohydrate foods with high GI values (70+) are quickly digested and converted into glucose (Often, these foods lack significant fiber content). Foods with medium GI values (55–70) become blood sugar at a medium rate. And low GI values (less than 55) are slowly absorbed. Low GI foods do not produce blood sugar spikes or stimulate the over-production of insulin. Guess where beans fit? In the low GI value range (30–40)! This makes them an excellent source of high-quality carbohydrates.

Low Glycemic Index (Less than 55)	Medium Glycemic Index (55–70)	High Glycemic Index (70+)
(41) Spaghetti	(67) Croissant	(72) Bagels
(53) 100% Stone-Ground Whole-Wheat	(69) Whole-Wheat Bread	(74) Graham Crackers
(54) Sweet Potato	(70) White Bread	(74) Saltine Crackers

Source: Brand-Miller J., Wolever T. *The Glucose Revolution: The Authoritative Guide to the Glycemic Index.* New York: Marlowe & Company, 1999.

While there have not been many studies conducted on bean intake and diabetes risk, a study of more than 65,000 nurses found that those consuming a diet of foods with higher GI values had more than *double* the risk of developing diabetes compared to those eating a diet of lower GI foods.[45]

HOW TO USE

There are many creative ways to add beans into your diet. Use Eden® Organic canned beans in salads, soups, chili, dips, casseroles, and burritos, and try the famous Woodstock Black Beans & Greens recipe that follows.

Beans can be yet another quick and healthy food to add to your diet. Experiment with the variety of dried and canned beans available today. There are several brands of canned beans in the natural foods market that have less sodium. Choose canned beans that are:

- Organically grown,
- Made with less than 150 milligrams sodium per serving, and are
- Made without added preservatives.

Hippie Wisdom

Woodstock Black Beans & Greens

1 tablespoon extra-virgin olive oil
1 teaspoon ground cumin
1 large onion, chopped
½ teaspoon of fresh ginger, minced
2 cloves garlic, minced
15-ounce can stewed tomatoes (or 2–3 fresh tomatoes, chopped)
4-ounce can diced green chilies
15-ounce can Eden Organic black beans

2 cups chopped collards, de-stemmed and cut into 2-inch pieces
⅓ cup nutritional yeast (see food category: *Nutritional Yeast*)
1 tablespoon fresh cilantro, chopped
1 teaspoon salt (taste before adding)
¼ teaspoon cayenne pepper (optional)
Dash of black pepper

1. Heat olive oil over medium-high heat in large skillet. Add cumin and let cook for 1 minute.
2. Add onions, ginger, and garlic, and sauté until tender.
3. Add tomatoes, green chilies. Reduce heat to medium and cook, uncovered, 6–8 minutes.
4. Stir in beans, collards, nutritional yeast, cilantro, salt, cayenne pepper (optional), and black pepper.
5. Cover and simmer for 8–10 minutes.

Serves 4

Nutrition Analysis per Serving: 210 calories, 4.5 grams fat, 0.5 grams saturated fat, 3 grams monounsaturated fat, 0.5 grams polyunsaturated fat, 14 grams protein, 34 grams carbohydrates, 12 grams fiber, 590 milligrams sodium

Other Noteworthy Nutrients per Serving (DV = Daily Value):

Vitamin C	— 60% DV	Selenium	— 20% DV
Folate	— 60% DV	Potassium	— 15% DV
Vitamin A	— 40% DV	Calcium	— 10% DV
Iron	— 20% DV	Magnesium	— 10% DV

Ginger Ale

Millions of Americans regularly drink ginger ale to settle an upset stomach. While this is not surprising given the evidence that ginger combats nausea, it is rather odd when you consider that today's supermarket ginger ale does not contain *any* actual ginger.

CANADA DRY® GINGER ALE* INGREDIENTS

Carbonated water, high fructose syrup and/or sugar, citric acid, natural flavors, sodium benzoate (preservative), caramel color

DID YOU KNOW?

The Irish are credited with inventing ginger ale in the mid–19th century. Canadian John McLaughlin developed the modern day version of Canada Dry Ginger Ale in 1907.

Imagine the ability of ginger ale to ease indigestion if you drank a brand that was actually made with ginger. Research reveals that in addition to relieving stomach aches, ginger offers several health benefits that give it a medicinal quality. Maybe that is why sales of fresh ginger, ginger tea, candied ginger, and yes, *real* ginger ale such as Reeds® Ginger Brew have steadily increased in the last decade.

About Reed's®

Reed's, a publicly-held corporation founded in 1989, makes high-quality ginger beverages the old-fashioned way. Like traditional brewers, it blends wholesome fresh ingredients in small batches.

Ordinary soft drinks, and even some "natural" sodas, are made by mixing water with inexpensive sweeteners, colorings, and flavorings. Soda manufacturers rely on flavor crystals and chemicals to create a consistent taste that is less expensive to produce. Reed's, on the other hand, brews their beverages from roots, herbs, spices, and fruits,

* Canada Dry is a registered trademark of Cadbury Beverages, Inc.

including fresh ginger root, and filtered water. There are no refined sugars, preservatives, or any artificial ingredient in Reed's beverages. This commitment to quality accounts for Reed's top-selling status in the natural foods industry. For more information on Reed's, visit http://www.reedsgingerbrew.com/

Reed's Ginger Brew®

Reed's makes six different kinds of ginger brew. Every batch has a slightly different flavor and "heat" depending on the ginger and other ingredients. The Extra Ginger Brew might have too much bite for you, or you may think it's just right. All of the ginger brews are sweetened by fruit juices alone or a variety of natural sweeteners including fructose, fruit juices, pineapple concentrate, and honey. The flavors, ginger content, and source of sweetener for each 12-ounce serving are:

- **Extra Ginger Brew:** 25 grams of fresh ginger root. Sweetened with fructose, pineapple concentrate, and honey.
- **Original Ginger Brew:** 17 grams of fresh ginger root. Sweetened with fructose, pineapple concentrate, and honey.
- **Premium Ginger Brew:** 17 grams of fresh ginger root. Sweetened with only honey and pineapple juice. Does not contain fructose.
- **Raspberry Ginger Brew:** 17 grams of fresh ginger root. Sweetened with fructose and raspberry juice (20% of volume).
- **Cherry Ginger Brew:** 17 grams of fresh ginger root. Sweetened with fructose and cherry juice (from concentrate).
- **Spiced Apple Brew:** 8 grams of fresh ginger root. Sweetened with fructose and apple juice (50% of volume).

NUTRITIONAL BENEFITS

The health conscious shopper has driven the growth of the natural soft drink market because he or she is concerned about the additives found in regular soda drinks. People have discovered that the primary additive is high fructose corn syrup, an inexpensive refined sugar that contributes no valuable vitamins or minerals into the diet. There is a recent theory that too much high fructose corn syrup in the diet contributes to obesity by stimulating new fat synthesis and inhibiting fullness signals.[46] The implications of this are significant when one considers that the average consumption of this sweetener has increased more than 1000% between 1970 and today. In addition to causing dental cavities, the excessive intake of refined sugars likely increases the risk for developing diabetes. Even many of the "natural sodas" on the market today are sweetened with high fructose corn syrup. Remember, even though there may be no additives in most natural sodas, those that do not contain fruit juice or other beneficial nutrients are still only *empty sugar calories*.

Reed's Ginger Brews are unique because they contain a significant amount of fresh ginger root. Plants of the ginger family have long been used for therapeutic purposes, including relief of headaches, cardiovascular protection, vertigo, stomach upset, morning sickness, menstrual pain, ulcers, loss of appetite, and rheumatoid arthritis as well as increasing sperm motility and offering protection against cancer. An ancient health system developed over thousands of years in India called Ayurveda extols the health benefits of ginger. One of the leading Ayurvedic doctors, Vasant Lad, says: "Ginger is perhaps the best and most *sattvic* (life-supporting) of the spices. It was called *vishwabhesaj*, the universal medicine." More recently scientific research has provided supporting evidence for some of these longstanding claims and while much of the research on the health benefits of ginger is still in its infancy, results are promising and deserve our attention.

 . Current evidence shows that the substance that gives ginger its flavor, *gingerol*, appears to inhibit the growth of human cancer cells. Another substance in ginger, *paradol*, is believed to block tumor growth. Gingerol and paradol both have antioxidant and anti-inflammatory properties.

Laboratory experiments have shown that the gingerols found in ginger root can inhibit the growth of the bacteria *Helicobacter pylori* (H. pylori).[47] Scientists believe that H. pylori is a primary agent associated with peptic ulcer disease and the development of stomach and colon cancer.

Ginger reduces the severity of nausea and vomiting related to pregnancy. In one well-designed study, women consuming a supplement with just one gram of ginger daily reported significantly less nausea and experienced fewer vomiting episodes.[48] There is controversy regarding the safety of ginger *supplements* during pregnancy but no concern for ginger consumed as food.

Reed's also makes Reed's Crystallized Ginger, a ginger candy that is custom-produced in the South Pacific Islands from ginger root and raw cane sugar. Crystallized ginger keeps well and is a great traveling companion to ward off nausea and motion sickness.

Ginger ale is great to keep on hand as a delicious treat, a mixer, and when needed, for its nausea combating properties. Remember: leading supermarket ginger ale brands do not contain *any* real ginger. When shopping for ginger ale, choose those that:

- Contain real ginger (see label),
- Are fruit-juice sweetened instead of sweetened with high fructose corn syrup, and
- Are preservative-free.

Hippie Wisdom

Tortilla Chips

Tortilla chips are second only to potato chips in the $20 billion snack food market in the United States. Snack foods such as chips are a lucrative product for their manufacturers because the ingredients to produce them—corn, potatoes, oil, and salt—are relatively inexpensive. As separate commodities, they sell for just a few cents per pound, but when these ingredients are blended and fried, snack chips sell for several dollars a bag. There is a science to prolonging the lifespan of a chip, and the longer the snack food can be kept "fresh"—through air-tight packaging and preservatives—the better chance it has to sell. Additionally, recipes are masterfully crafted. We have all seen the commercial that boasts: "Betcha Can't Eat Just One!"* The ad hits home; the manufacturer's labs have engineered the most irresistible chips possible.

We need to remember our bottom line health concerns. We all know that tortilla chips are not regarded as "health food." Why then would I have chosen to include them among the best natural foods in the market? The reason is a practical one: Most of us do eat snack chips as a regular part of our diet and because I believe snack foods do not have to be bad for us. Sure, I'd rather see my clients eat almonds, but fortunately there are nutritionally superior chips on the market today.

There are companies, such as Kettle Foods®, that use organic ingredients and better-quality oils in their snack foods. They make a line of chips that deliver the same flavor (or better) than most chips, and they do so using wholesome ingredients. Eating chips in moderation . . . well, that part is up to us.

About Kettle Foods®

The first Kettle Foods potato chips hit the market in Salem, Oregon in 1982. These classic, natural, hand-cooked chips were made with only

---

* Slogan created in 1963 by Frito-Lay, Inc.

premium Russet potatoes grown on small family-owned farms in the Pacific Northwest. In 1992, the success of these potato chips led to the development of a premium tortilla chip made from scratch using organically grown corn. In 1997, the present day Kettle brand Tortilla Chips were launched. For more information on Kettle tortilla chips, visit http://www.kettlefoods.com/

Kettle Sesame Blue Moons® Tortilla Chips

Kettle makes Sesame Blue Moons with all non-GMO ingredients (see Section Three: *Genetically Engineered Foods*) including organic blue corn and organic safflower and/or sunflower oil. First, Kettle cooks the organically-grown corn slowly to maximize flavor, and then grinds it into masa dough. Next comes Kettle's special patented process: Kettle blends sprouted corn into the dough mixture to add natural sweetness, a key step that makes these chips unique. Finally, the production team shapes the chips and roasts them in high-monounsaturated organic safflower or sunflower oil, lightly salts, and packages them for market.

DID YOU KNOW?

In November, 2003, the Kettle Foods potato chip production line in Salem, Oregon became solar powered. The roof brought solar power to the Northwest's largest industrial solar installation. During peak solar hours, the system will contribute 25% of the company's electricity demand. The power generated over the next 25 years will be enough to produce six million bags of snack chips … and save energy bills, too.

NUTRITIONAL BENEFITS

While good nutrition and chips are not often discussed in the same sentence, the tortilla chips made by Kettle Foods are far healthier than the leading supermarket brands. The three main considerations are:

- The quality of ingredients
- The type of oil used
- The addition of preservatives, if any

The Importance of Reading the Ingredients List (A Bit of Hippie Wisdom)

When you pick up a bag of snack chips, take a peek at the ingredient list. Does the food contain any whole foods such as corn, oats, or whole-wheat flour? Are any of the ingredients listed as *organic*? Compare the ingredients of any one of Kettle Foods brands (see below) with a leading supermarket brand. The whole foods in the Sesame Blue Moons are blue corn and sesame seeds. Both the grains *and* oil were grown organically. Furthermore, the ingredients in Kettle chips are made without genetic engineering (GMO).

Next, notice the type of oil used to make the snack chips. As you probably know, the hydrogenated oils found in many processed foods are the most harmful oils you can eat. Beyond the fact that these trans fats are bad news, pesticide concentrations in some commercially-produced oils, such as cottonseed oil, are toxic. Choose a product with organic oil to reduce your exposure to environmental contaminants. Know that the refining process strips commercially-produced polyunsaturated oils, such as cottonseed, soybean, corn, and safflower oils of their natural substances (like antioxidants) that actually make the oil healthier for your body. Read the ingredient list to help you identify and choose products that use expeller-pressed oils rather than those extracted with chemical solvents (see Section Three: *Fats & Oils*). Many natural food manufacturers are using more stable oils (less likely to spoil) that are also high in heart-healthy monounsaturated fats (oleic fats). These oils include: olive oil, high-oleic sunflower, and high-oleic safflower (see Section Three: *Fats & Oils*).

KETTLE SESAME BLUE MOONS

> Organically grown blue corn, sesame seeds, sprouted organically grown blue corn, organic expeller-pressed high-monounsaturated safflower and/or sunflower oil, salt

LEADING SUPERMARKET BRAND

> Corn, vegetable oil (one or more: corn, sunflower, or soybean oil), cheddar cheese, salt, buttermilk solids, wheat flour, whey, protein

concentrate, Romano cheese, tomato powder, monosodium glutamate (MSG), onion powder, partially hydrogenated soybean oil, whey, garlic powder, dextrose, sugar, disodium phosphate, lactic acid, natural flavor, spice, citric acid, parmesan cheese, artificial colors (includes yellow 6, red 40), disodium inosinate, disodium guanylate

There may be additives and preservatives in your chips that are unhealthy for you. This is the last useful piece of information that you can glean from the ingredient list. Without being an expert on additives (see Section Three: *Food Additives*), you can trust Kettle brand chips. Moreover, *most* natural foods producers do not rely on artificial flavorings and preservatives in the manufacturing process.

NUTRITIONAL BENEFITS

Nutrients	Leading Supermarket Brand 1 oz (28 g)	Kettle Sesame Blue Moons 1 oz. (28 g) 15 chips
Calories	140	150
Total Fat	7 grams	8 grams
Saturated Fat	1 grams	0.5 grams
Trans Fat	< 0.5 grams	No
Sodium	110 milligrams	80 milligrams

As you will find when you start reading ingredient lists, most supermarket chips are made with non-organic grains, less healthy oils, and additives. Often, using only the nutrition information on the label (see above), it is hard to distinguish one product from another. Remember, quality foods can *only* be made using quality ingredients.

Tortilla chips are great for the right occasion. Do yourself a favor, though, and buy healthier snack chips. Check out the list of ingredients. Steer clear of hydrogenated oils and weird-sounding preservatives. I suggest that you choose brands made with healthier oils and simple ingredients.

Hippie Wisdom

Groovy Guacamole

1 ripe avocado
Juice of ½ large lime
1 clove garlic, minced
1 tablespoon sliced scallions
¼ cup chopped red pepper
1 large fresh tomato, chopped
½ cup frozen organic green peas, thawed

1 tablespoon Bragg Liquid Aminos® (see food category: *Soy Sauce Alternative*)
1 tablespoon chopped fresh cilantro
½ teaspoon salt
Dash of pepper

1. Mash avocado with food processor or fork to desired consistency.
2. Combine all ingredients in a serving dish.
3. Chill before serving.
4. Store covered for up to 3 days.

Serves 8

Serving Size: ½ cup

Nutrition Analysis per Serving: 60 calories, 4 grams fat, 0.5 gram saturated fat, 2.5 grams monounsaturated fat, 0.5 grams polyunsaturated fat, 3 grams protein, 2 grams carbohydrates, 2 grams fiber, 320 milligrams sodium

Other Noteworthy Nutrients per Serving (DV = Daily Value):
Vitamin C — 30% DV
Vitamin A — 10% DV
(as beta carotene)

Salsa

Tomatoes are one of most valuable vegetable crops in the U.S. Where do all those little tomatoes go? If you guessed into a ketchup bottle, you may be surprised to learn that salsa has surpassed ketchup as the top-selling condiment. The growing Hispanic population in the U.S., as well as the popularity of Mexican food in general, has boosted salsa sales in recent years.

Salsa is the Spanish word for "sauce." I like to prepare it using fresh raw ingredients (salsa cruda), but most commercial salsas are prepared with ingredients that are cooked. A misconception is that salsa is only *red* (salsa roja), but salsa comes in other colors. There is the wonderful green salsa (salsa verde) made from tomatillos (a small green tomato), cilantro, and green chili peppers that you will find in many delis, restaurants, and natural foods markets. If you are lucky, you may even find orange and yellow salsas that derive their color from fresh tropical fruits such as mango, papaya, and pineapples.

There are many health benefits to selecting salsa made from quality ingredients, but most salsas in the supermarket consist of little more than tomato puree, a few chopped vegetables, vinegar, and preservatives. Fortunately, natural food markets offer a variety of salsa products that are made using delicious natural ingredients. One line of flavorful salsas that tastes freshly prepared is made by Frontera Foods®. The many different products that this company puts out consist of a variety of peppers and other natural ingredients.

> **DID YOU KNOW?**
>
> The chemical in hot peppers that gives them a spicy kick is called *capsaicin*. Preliminary evidence suggests that capsaicin is protective against ulcers and can prevent damage to the stomach caused by aspirin and other non-steroidal anti-inflammatory medications.

About Frontera Foods®

In 1987, after six years of culinary research in Mexico, chef Rick Bayless*, whose credits include hosting the PBS television series *Mexico—One Plate at a Time*, opened the Frontera Grill in Chicago, Illinois. The Frontera Grill specializes in contemporary regional Mexican cooking and has been, from the start, a smash hit, leading to the formation of Frontera Foods in 1996. Frontera produces authentic Mexican food products including salsa. For more information on Frontera salsas, visit http://www.fronterakitchens.com/

Frontera® Classic Salsas

Frontera salsas are made in small batches that are fire-roasted to concentrate, sweeten, and intensify the flavors of the natural ingredients. There are nine different varieties from which to choose:

Roasted Tomato Salsa with fresh cilantro and mild red chiles
Roasted Red Pepper and Garlic Salsa with roasted tomatoes
Tomatillo Salsa with serrano chiles, roasted onions, and cilantro
Rustic Gaujillo Salsa with tangy tomatillos and garlic
Roasted Poblano Salsa with fresh tomatoes and salsa
Jalapeno Cilantro Salsa with roasted tomatoes and garlic
Chipotle Salsa with mellow garlic and smoky roasted tomatillos
Tangy Two-Chile Salsa with roasted tomatoes and tomatillos
Habanero Salsa with roasted tomatoes and cilantro

Frontera makes all their salsas with simple, natural ingredients, and no added preservatives or artificial flavors. The ingredients of **Habanero Salsa**, for example, are: tomatoes, onions, water, habanero chiles, cilantro, fresh garlic, salt, and paprika.

---

* Bayless has written several books including *Salsas That Cook*. He is the past chairman of Chefs Collaborative 2000, in support of environmentally-sound agricultural practices. Bayless is currently active in *Share Our Strength*, the nation's largest hunger advocacy organization.

NUTRITIONAL BENEFITS

In 1998, the USDA officially declared salsa a vegetable and thus eligible for reimbursement under the National School Lunch Program. Revered as a condiment, salsa is much more than ketchup, and for only a few calories, it provides some real nutritional value. Two tablespoons of Frontera salsa provides 6%–10% of the daily requirement of vitamin C, as well as up to 4% of the daily requirement for vitamin A. Even greater benefits may be found in the phytochemicals (plant-based chemicals) contained in the variety of peppers, tomatoes, tomatillos, garlic, and cilantro.

One powerful antioxidant called *lycopene* is found in tomatoes. To date, 35 studies have shown a positive relationship between blood lycopene levels and the reduced risk of developing cancer.[49] Research shows that lycopene is best absorbed from cooked tomato products like salsa. In a study of more than 700 women (289 with breast cancer, 442 without), the dietary intake of lycopene was estimated. Researchers found that those consuming the most lycopene in the control group—primarily from tomato-based products—had a 36% reduced risk of developing breast cancer. These results held true even after factoring out six other nutrients known to protect against breast cancer.[50] Similarly for men, regular consumption of lycopene is linked with a reduced incidence of prostate cancer. In a 13-year case-control study of nearly 600 men, some with prostate cancer and some without, controls with the highest intake of lycopene had a 60% reduced risk of developing prostate cancer.[51] In addition to *preventing* prostate cancer, there is evidence that lycopene provides benefits even after a person has cancer. Thirty-two patients with localized prostate cancer were fed a tomato sauce-rich diet (providing 30 milligrams of lycopene daily)* for three weeks prior to surgery. The increased tomato sauce intake resulted in a significant reduction in prostate tissue damage and PSA (prostate specific antigen) levels compared to pre-intervention levels.[52] In addition to lycopene, other carotenoids in tomatoes such as *phytofluene* and *zeta-carotene*, reduce prostate cancer cell growth in laboratory tests.[53]

*Two tablespoons of Frontera Roasted Tomato Salsa contains 4–6 milligrams of lycopene.

Hippie Wisdom

Salsa is a great addition to a meal. Try it with scrambled eggs, on toast, in a salad, or on a serving of quinoa (see food category: *Quinoa*). Just make sure you are eating the good stuff! Look for salsas that contain:

- Natural ingredients, like tomatoes, garlic, cilantro, onions, and peppers,
- Organic ingredients, and
- No artificial flavorings or preservatives.

Spelt

One of the earliest grains grown by farmers as far back as 5,000 B.C. was spelt (*Triticum spelta*), a cousin to modern wheat (*Triticum aestivum*). Spelt is native to southern Europe and has been, because of its delicious nutty flavor and excellent baking properties, a long-time favorite among Europeans. Bread made from spelt flour is quickly being discovered by Americans as a satisfying alternative to less nutritious white breads. Spelt offers many of the same nutritious benefits of other whole grains, has a great taste, and is lighter and fluffier in texture than whole-wheat. A real plus is that spelt is also better tolerated by those with wheat sensitivities.

> **DID YOU KNOW?**
>
> Spelt has a tougher husk making it more difficult to process than modern wheat varieties. This husk actually protects against insects making it an easier crop to grow organically.

Not yet in most supermarkets, spelt breads, spelt flour, and baked goods made from spelt are now available in most natural foods stores. If you have never eaten spelt, I highly recommend that you try a loaf of spelt bread the next time you visit the bakery section. For the more ambitious who are interested in baking their own spelt bread, a leading brand of spelt flour is packaged and sold by Bob's Red Mill®.

About Bob's Red Mill®

When Bob Moore read *John Goffe's Mill* by George Woodbury, he was struck with the idea of establishing an old-fashioned mill and producing natural foods in a traditional way. With the help of his wife Charlee, he sought a quartz millstone of the highest quality. An exhaustive search paid off with the discovery of an existing set of 19th century French millstones in North Carolina, which the couple hauled across the country to begin their milling operation in California.

Despite the sophistication of the modern era, the Moores believe that no machinery—none of the hammer mills, high-speed steel roller mills, or pulverizers commonly used today—can grind grains into better baking bread flour than the old quartz millstones, and time has shown that instinct to be true. Today, Bob's Red Mill grinds a wide variety of flours and produces an extensive selection of unique cereals, pancake, waffle, and bread mixes, and specialty grain products that have become some of the company's best-selling products. For more information on Bob's Red Mill, visit http://www.bobsredmill.com/

Spelt Flour

Spelt flour is made by grinding spelt berries into flour. Like wheat, spelt flour can be made from the entire spelt berry (whole-spelt flour) or can be made from just the starchy component without the bran and germ (white spelt flour). *White* spelt flour—or a mixture of whole-spelt and white spelt—is often used to replace regular white flour.

NUTRITIONAL BENEFITS

Spelt is a whole grain that offers many of the same nutritional benefits found in whole-wheat including high-fiber, B-vitamins, magnesium, and manganese. Like other whole plant foods, spelt and products made from spelt flour contain other plant chemicals—such as phenols, lignans and flavonoids—that offer health benefits. Baked goods made with refined white flour, or even white spelt flour, lack the *bran* and *germ* containing the majority of vitamins, minerals, and plant chemicals in whole grain bread (see Section Three: *Wheat Products*).

The available nutrients that we lose when we choose a slice of white bread instead of a slice of whole-spelt bread are:

90% Vitamin E	75% Zinc
85% Vitamin B_6	60% Copper
80% Magnesium	40% Folate
80% Manganese	

For the previous reasons, many of my clients (whether they suspect that they are sensitive to wheat or not) are choosing whole-spelt bread and products made with spelt flour as healthier alternatives (see Section Three: *Wheat Products*).

How to Use

Whole-spelt flour is an excellent flour substitute for any recipe that calls for white or whole-wheat flour. Spelt and spelt flour is used to make cereals, pastas, crackers, baked goods, and beer.

Give spelt bread a try, and look for whole-spelt bread instead of white spelt bread. Spelt breads cost more than regular bread unless you make it yourself. When baking at home, try replacing white flour with whole-spelt flour (see recipe that follows). In summary:

- Spelt is a healthy, nutritious grain with great baking properties, and
- Replacing some wheat in your diet with spelt and other grains can help improve wheat tolerance.

Hippie Wisdom

Summer of Love Spelt Bread

1½ cups warm water
4 teaspoons baking yeast
4 tablespoons honey
1 tablespoon extra-virgin olive oil

1 cup whole-wheat bread flour (can be replaced by 1 cup whole-spelt)
3 cups Bob's Red Mill whole-spelt flour
½ cup flaxseeds, ground
1 teaspoon salt

1. Place warm water (not hot) in a bowl. Evenly distribute the yeast by sprinkling on top of the water. Drizzle two tablespoons of honey into the bowl. Add ½ tablespoon olive oil and stir gently with a fork to incorporate the honey.

2. Let rest for several minutes until yeast is visibly active (has a layer of froth).

3. Separately, mix the whole-wheat bread flour, spelt flour, ground flaxseed, and salt in a large bowl. In cooler weather, ingredients should be mixed in a bowl that has been warmed slightly to keep the yeast active.

4. When yeast mixture is ready, add to the flour mixture along with the other 2 tablespoons of honey and the other ½ tablespoon of olive oil.

5. Mix ingredients thoroughly. Add a small amount of spelt flour to the mixture if the ingredients stick to your hands. Add a small amount of water if the mixture is too dry. Knead thoroughly by hand or with a mixer for 7–10 minutes.

6. Place dough into a clean, lightly oiled bowl, cover with a damp cloth, and let rise in a draft-free place. After it has doubled in size, punch down, knead gently for several more minutes, and place into a greased bread pan. Let rise again until it is loaf size.

7. Bake in a preheated oven at 375 degrees for 20–25 minutes until done.

Serves 12

Nutrition Analysis per Serving: 190 calories, 3.5 grams fat, 0 grams saturated fat, 1.5 grams monounsaturated fat, 2 grams polyunsaturated fat, 6 grams protein, 39 grams carbohydrates, 8 grams fiber, 190 milligrams sodium

Other Noteworthy Nutrients per Serving (DV = Daily Value):
Omega–3s (ALA) — 1 gram
Iron — 10% DV
Selenium — 10% DV

Tempeh

Tempeh is a traditional Indonesian food dating back more than 2,000 years. It is a fermented, cake-like product made from soybeans alone or soybeans with grains such as millet, rice, or barley. Tempeh is cultured by a mold called *Rhizopus oligosporus*. (Do not worry; the mold is as harmless as that used to make blue cheese.) The tempeh process begins with cleansed soybeans that are then cooked, lightly ground, and made into patties. The mold culture is added and incubated at 85°F–95°F for 24 hours. At this point, a white filament-like substance called *mycelia* covers the mixture and binds it together. The tempeh is then packaged into cakes, pasteurized, refrigerated or frozen, and sent to market.

Tempeh is growing in popularity in many top-notch restaurants and markets. It has a pleasant nutty taste that complements other flavors in a cooked dish (try a recipe that uses tempeh in a stir-fry) and is one of the healthiest soy foods on the market today (see Section Three: *Soy Products*). Besides gaining the benefits of soy, when you choose tempeh, you also win by displacing the less-healthy protein foods in your diet such as red meat. A leading producer of tempeh using the highest quality ingredients is Lightlife Foods®.

About Lightlife Foods®

Tempeh Works® first opened its doors in 1979. By 1982 it had introduced its first tempeh burger, the Tamari Grille, and by 1984 had grown into Lightlife Foods. Continuing to expand, the company introduced a full new array of soy-based products, and today Lightlife Foods remains committed to providing the best 100% natural, 100% vegetarian products available. All Lightlife tempeh products are made from organically-grown, non-GMO soybeans (see Section Three: *Genetically Engineered Foods*) and contain no artificial ingredients. The tempeh products all are considered kosher and vegan. Vegan means that the tempeh does not contain and was not processed using any animal products. For more information on Lightlife tempeh, visit http://www.lightlife.com/

NUTRITIONAL BENEFITS

Tempeh is a nutritional powerhouse! It is low in calories and fat and completely free of cholesterol. Calorie for calorie it offers as much protein as beef. Mild in flavor, tempeh is a good source of fiber, vitamin E, and iron and is easy to digest. It is during tempeh's fermentation process that enzymes are activated to make the soybean more digestible. Many of my clients who have difficulty digesting beans have no problem with tempeh. Compare the nutritional differences between 200 calories of beef, chicken, and tempeh below.

Nutrients	Beef Prime Filet Mignon (2.5 oz.)	Chicken Light Meat w/o skin (4 oz.)	Lightlife Organic Tempeh–Soy (4 oz.)
Calories	220	200	210
Total Fat	17 grams	5 grams	9 grams
Saturated Fat	7 grams (30% Daily Value)	1.5 grams	1 gram
Myristic Acid	0.5 grams	0 grams	0 grams
Fiber	0 grams	0 grams	10 grams (50% DV)
Protein	18 grams	33 grams	19 grams
Isoflavones	0 milligrams	0 milligrams	60 milligrams
Iron	2.2 milligrams	1.2 milligrams	3 milligrams

Here you see that the most significant differences are in total fat, saturated fat, fiber, and isoflavone content. Lightlife Organic Tempeh provides a whopping 10 grams of fiber, or nearly half of the recommended daily intake. Isoflavones are plant estrogens (see Section Three: *Soy Products*) that may well be protective against certain forms of cancer. In addition, isoflavones improve the functioning of arteries,[54] a cardiovascular benefit independent of the cholesterol-lowering effects of these plant estrogens.

HOW TO USE

Do not be alarmed if you notice discoloration such as black or gray spots on the tempeh; like cheese, this is only a natural part of the fermentation process. Once opened, tempeh keeps for four days when covered and can be frozen for up to six months. Because all Lightlife tempeh products are pasteurized before they are sold, you can snack on them directly from the package or cook them (baked, broiled, steamed, or pan-fried). Try adding cubed tempeh to stir-fry dishes, crumbling it on pizzas, adding it in chili, lasagna, or stews, or slicing it for sandwiches.

If tempeh is a new food for you, I recommend that you first try it in a good restaurant. You can find it on the menu in many Asian-style, vegetarian, or other progressive restaurants. When buying tempeh at a natural foods market, look for those made with organic, non-GMO soybeans. Try tempeh products that are already marinated and ready to eat.

Hippie Wisdom

Diggin' On Tempeh

2 tablespoons extra-virgin olive oil

2 cloves garlic, chopped

1 medium green pepper, cored and chopped

8 ounces Lightlife Organic Soy Tempeh, cut into ½-inch cubes

2 tablespoons Bragg Liquid Aminos® (see food category: *Soy Sauce Alternative*)

1. Heat olive oil over medium-high heat in large skillet.
2. Sauté garlic and green pepper. Do not burn (the oil should not emit smoke).
3. Add tempeh and Bragg Liquid Aminos.
4. Cook for 6–8 minutes, stirring to avoid charring.
5. Serve with rice, in tortillas, on spelt toast, or with salad greens.

Serves 2

Nutrition Analysis per Serving: 330 calories, 20 grams fat, 3 grams saturated fat, 12 grams monounsaturated fat, 3 grams polyunsaturated fat, 25 grams protein, 14 grams carbohydrates, 8 grams fiber, 660 milligrams sodium

Other Noteworthy Nutrients per Serving (DV = Daily Value):

Vitamin C	— 90% DV	Calcium	— 20% DV
Magnesium	— 25% DV	Potassium	— 15% DV
Iron	— 20% DV	Folate	— 15% DV

Tahini

A delight from the Middle East, tahini is a thick peanut-butter-like paste that is made from ground sesame seeds. The most popular tahini-based foods available in delicatessens and natural food stores are hummus and the eggplant spread called baba ghanoush. After some experimentation with tahini at home and in restaurants, you may, like many, grow to love the creaminess that it adds to food. You may even discover a favorite new salad dressing.

Why Add Tahini to Your Diet?

Tahini's most obvious contribution to one's diet is the delicious flavor it lends to foods; but don't forget, too, that research consistently finds health benefits from the *regular* consumption of nuts and seeds (see Section Three: *Fats & Oils*).

DID YOU KNOW?

Sesame seeds are actually the first recorded seasoning, dating back to Assyria in 3000 B.C.

One study found that when people ate sesame seeds, their plasma level of *gamma tocopherol* (a potent form of vitamin E) increased far more than when they ate equal amounts of gamma tocopherol from walnuts or soybean oil.[55] These findings are consistent with animal studies correlating sesame seeds with increased vitamin E activity in the body. Another noteworthy point is that sesame seeds contain plant estrogens called *lignans*. These compounds, and in particular *sesamin*, have antioxidant properties and may protect against cancer and heart disease. Additionally, foods containing tahini, such as hummus and lemon tahini salad dressing, can be chosen to replace less healthy fat sources such as butter and certain oil-based dressings (see comparison on page 131). Like other nut and seed butters, the majority of fat calories in tahini is derived from a heart-healthier *unsaturated* fat.

Beyond the cardiovascular benefits, tahini provides a significant source of calcium, protein, iron, magnesium, and other little-known plant chemicals. Imagine getting *real* nutrition from your salad dressing.

Nutrients	Ranch Dressing (soybean oil) (2 tablespoons)	Lay It On Me! Lemon Tahini Dressing (see page 132) (2 tablespoons)
Calories	240	80
Protein	0 grams	2 grams
Saturated fat	2 grams	1 grams
Myristic Acid	0 grams	0 grams
Calcium, Folate, Magnesium, Iron, Vitamin C	None	2%–10% Daily Value
Phytochemicals	Trace	Good Source

How Do I Use Tahini?

While you may find that tahini by itself has a slightly bitter taste, when combined with other ingredients like garbanzo beans, salt, and lemon juice to make hummus, you get a tasty dip and spread. A popular use of tahini in restaurants is in lemon tahini salad dressing (see recipe that follows). Tahini also greatly enhances the flavor and texture of casseroles, dips, and sauces.

Tahini is a great food to add into your diet. It's healthy and can be delicious when prepared properly. Try ordering lemon tahini dressing the next time you see it on a menu. Tahini can often be found in supermarkets and specialty stores in the ethnic or foreign food aisle. Look for tahini products, roasted or raw, made from organic sesame seeds.

Hippie Wisdom

Lay It On Me! Lemon Tahini Dressing

½ cup Woodstock Farms® organic tahini

⅓ cup lemon juice

2 garlic cloves, minced (note: use less garlic for mild flavor)

2 tablespoons Bragg Liquid Aminos® (see food category: *Soy Sauce Alternative*)

½ teaspoon basil, dried

½ teaspoon garlic powder

¼ teaspoon salt

Dash of cayenne (optional)

Dash of black pepper (optional)

Water

1. In a blender, mix all ingredients until smooth.
2. Add water to desired consistency.
3. Store refrigerated in a container with a tight-fitting lid.

Note: Dressing thickens as it sits and with refrigeration.

Serves 8

Serving Size: 2 tablespoons

Nutrition Analysis per Serving: 80 calories, 6.5 grams fat, 0.9 grams saturated fat, 2.5 grams monounsaturated fat, 3 grams polyunsaturated fat, 2.5 grams protein, 3.5 grams carbohydrates, 0.5 grams fiber, 170 milligrams sodium

Other Noteworthy Nutrients per Serving (DV = Daily Value):
Vitamin C   —   10% DV

Quinoa

Have you heard of the super grain *quinoa*? If you haven't, you might not be quite sure what to make of this impressive food. Quinoa (pronounced KEEN-wah) is an ivory-colored seed from a grass native to the Andes Mountains of South America and was a staple food of the ancient Incas. While it is grown in the mountainous regions of Colorado and Canada, the majority of the available quinoa today still comes from Bolivia, Ecuador, and Peru.

> **DID YOU KNOW?**
>
> Colorado has an environment similar to Bolivia, where quinoa originated. Unlike most grains, quinoa can grow well at elevations between 7,000 and 11,000 feet.

Quinoa is not a hard sell. When eaten by first-timers, it is readily enjoyed and becomes a favorite. Like cous cous, quinoa has a delicate taste and light, almost nutty, flavor. It is an excellent grain to use in dishes that call for white or brown rice. Unlike many whole grains that take close to an hour to prepare, quinoa cooks in only 15–20 minutes.

Quinoa is a good source of valuable nutrients. As more Americans learn about the benefits of this grain, the availability of products containing it surely will increase. An excellent source of organic quinoa grown in Ecuador is packaged and sold in natural foods stores by Bob's Red Mill® (see Spelt: About Bob's Red Mill).

About Bob's Red Mill®

In the 1980s, Bob Moore recognized a need in the marketplace for flour produced in a natural way. His company, Bob's Red Mill, started small with just a few products and today produces more than 400 different foods. Many of the grains that are packaged in its facility are unusual whole grains like quinoa, teff, amaranth, and kamut. Bob's Red Mill sells more than 40 different organic products under the company label, including organic quinoa grown in Ecuador. For more information on Bob's Red Mill, visit http://www.bobsredmill.com/

NUTRITIONAL BENEFITS

If you are looking for a good source of protein you can find it in a grain: indeed, amazingly, quinoa is considered a *complete protein*. Francis Moore Lappe's *Diet for a Small Planet*, written back in the "Hippie Wisdom Days" of 1971, brought this to our awareness. She taught us how to make sure we were getting complete proteins from our plant foods by eating *complementary proteins*. Virtually all plant foods lack an adequate level of at least one of the essential amino acids to be a complete protein on their own. However, a plant food lacking one amino acid can be combined with a plant food lacking a different amino acid, thus forming a "complete protein." (Try eating, for example, a plate of beans and rice for a complete protein.) Since the idea of complementary proteins came to the fore, researchers have learned that the body can make complete proteins from different plant foods eaten not just in one dish but throughout the course of an entire day. When eating quinoa, you don't have to think twice about protein because with this super grain, it's all there.

Quinoa offers more than protein. It also is a good source of vitamins and minerals. A ¾ cup serving of cooked quinoa provides 25% of the daily value for both iron and magnesium and 10% of the daily value for vitamin E, potassium, and fiber. And, I suspect there are beneficial plant chemicals in quinoa still to be discovered. In the meantime, it is safe to extrapolate from other studies regarding whole grains. A higher dietary intake of whole grains lowers your risk for diabetes, heart disease, and certain cancers. Compare the nutritional advantages of choosing quinoa over white rice as a fast-cooking grain for dinner (see below).

Nutrients	Long-Grain White Rice, enriched (¾ cup cooked)	Quinoa (¾ cup cooked)
Calories	200	200
Fat	0 grams	3 grams
Saturated Fat	0 grams	0 grams
Protein	3 grams	7 grams
Fiber	< 1 gram	3 grams
Iron	10% Daily Value (DV)	25% Daily Value (DV)
Magnesium	5% DV	25% DV
Potassium	2% DV	10% DV

How to Use

Quinoa contains a phytochemical called *saponin*, found mainly on the surface of the seed. It is believed that the plant produces saponins, which have a bitter taste, to discourage birds and insects from eating it. Most quinoa sold in the United States has already been cleansed of saponin. Still, to reduce the risk of any bitterness, you can rinse the grain briefly in a strainer under hot water before cooking.

Use two cups of water to every one cup of dry quinoa. As mentioned, you can cook quinoa in a short 15-20 minutes. When fully cooked, quinoa is fluffy and has a white spiral halo attached to each seed.

Try quinoa in pilafs, casseroles, soups, and as a base for stir-fried vegetables or beans. Quinoa flour and pastas made from quinoa are also available in many natural food stores.

Quinoa is a really *cool* food to add into your regular diet. At least try it if you've never tasted it before. Look for it on the menu at progressive restaurants. Quinoa is sold packaged and in the bulk section of natural food stores.

Hippie Wisdom

Cosmic Quinoa Salad

1 cup Bob's Red Mill quinoa, rinsed

2 cups water

1 medium or large tomato, cut into ½ inch cubes

6 green onions, finely chopped

1 medium cucumber, peeled and cut into ½ inch pieces

1 small red pepper, seeded and cut into ½ inch pieces

½ cup finely-chopped fresh cilantro

⅓ cup freshly squeezed lemon juice

¼ cup extra-virgin olive oil

1¼ teaspoons salt

1. Put the quinoa in a fine strainer and thoroughly rinse with hot water to remove saponins.

2. In a medium saucepan, bring the quinoa and the water to a boil over high heat.

3. Reduce the heat to low, cover, and simmer until the quinoa is tender and the water is absorbed, 12 to 15 minutes. Transfer the quinoa to a large bowl.

4. Mix the tomato, green onion, cucumber, red pepper, and cilantro into the quinoa.

5. In a small bowl, whisk together the lemon juice, olive oil, and salt. Pour over the quinoa and toss well. Cover and refrigerate for at least 30 minutes before serving.

Serves 7

Serving Size: 1 cup

Nutrition Analysis per Serving: 180 calories, 10 grams fat, 1.5 grams saturated fat, 7 grams monounsaturated fat, 1.5 grams polyunsaturated fat, 4 grams protein, 24 grams carbohydrates, 2 grams fiber, 390 milligrams sodium

Other Noteworthy Nutrients per Serving (DV = Daily Value):

Vitamin C — 60% DV
Magnesium — 15% DV
Iron — 15% DV
Potassium — 10% DV

Soy Sauce Alternative

Americans consume on average fifteen pounds of salt every year. The heavy reliance on salt for improving the taste of food makes it the second leading food additive after sugar. While the medical field has long advised us to moderately reduce sodium intake, the latest guidelines released by the Institute of Medicine in 2004 are quite restrictive. To stay healthy, we are now advised to consume no more than 1,500 to 2,300 milligrams of sodium per day.

It is surprisingly easy to reach the upper limit of this guideline in a single meal when one teaspoon of salt has 2,400 milligrams of sodium. Studies indicate that the average person surpasses 4,000 milligrams of sodium each day, the majority of which finds its way into our mouths from restaurant meals and processed foods.

Along with table salt, another popular sodium-rich condiment is soy sauce, to which Americans were introduced through Chinese food. Today, we know that the liberal usage of soy sauce in traditional Chinese cuisine makes this ethnic food notoriously high in sodium. Another sodium-rich liquid concentrate similar to soy sauce that is also available in many stores and restaurants is called tamari. Originating in Japan, tamari is a little thicker than soy sauce and is commonly used in stir-fries and to season rice, potatoes, casseroles, pasta sauces, and salad dressings.

DID YOU KNOW?

Too much sodium can contribute to elevated blood pressure. The lack of potassium (a mineral found in whole-foods such as bananas, beans, and spinach) exacerbates the relationship between sodium and blood pressure.

The high sodium content of soy sauce and tamari has created a market for lower-sodium alternatives. Lite soy sauce and lite tamari are available in markets today, but I think they both taste watered down. One lower-sodium choice that is delicious and flavorful is Bragg Liquid Aminos® (see on page 138). Like other health enthusiasts, I have been a fan of "Braggs" for many years.

About Bragg Live Foods®

Paul C. Bragg, a true health pioneer since 1912, founded Bragg Live Foods. The company is now operated by daughter Patricia Bragg, a naturopathic physician and health enthusiast. She spreads the message of nutritional well-being through numerous informative books and company literature that support the Bragg product line, which currently includes organic apple cider vinegar, organic olive oil, and Bragg Liquid Aminos. For more information on Bragg Live Foods, visit http://www.bragg.com/

Bragg Liquid Aminos®

Bragg Liquid Aminos is a liquid concentrate, similar to soy sauce, made from non-genetically modified (GMO) soybeans. "Braggs" is used to enhance the flavor of a wide variety of foods. It contains no artificial colorings, no alcohol, and no preservatives.

BRAGG LIQUID AMINOS INGREDIENTS:

  Non-GMO soybeans and purified water

NUTRITIONAL BENEFITS

Unlike soy sauce and tamari, Bragg Liquid Aminos does not contain any wheat, salt, or other additives. Compare the sodium differences and ingredients of these three soy-based condiments below.

	Soy Sauce 1 tablespoon	Tamari 1 tablespoon	Bragg Liquid Aminos 1 tablespoon
Sodium	1000 milligrams	960 milligrams	660 milligrams
Ingredients	Water, soybeans, wheat, salt	Water, soybeans, salt, alcohol (to preserve freshness), wheat	Formulated soy protein from non-GMO soybeans and purified water

Clearly, one easy way to lower sodium intake is to use Bragg Liquid Aminos where soy sauce or tamari is called for. Another way is to use more spices (such as basil, oregano, and cumin), flavorful foods (ginger,

Soy Sauce
Alternative

onions, peppers, mushrooms, lemon, and lime), and condiments naturally low in sodium (including balsamic vinegar and some hot sauces).

How to Use

The flavor of Bragg Liquid Aminos works well with salad dressings, stir-fries, soups, sauces, casseroles, potatoes, rice, tofu and tempeh dishes, and poultry and fish as well as on cooked vegetables and popcorn.

After eating healthier foods, your taste buds will truly start coming back to life! You simply won't need to use as much salt on your food. Start adding a variety of flavorful spices, fresh and dried, to your food to make it more delicious. Try adding a squirt of Bragg Liquid Aminos *after* you've tasted your food if you need a flavor boost.

Hippie Wisdom

Flower Child Cucumber Salad

1 large red, yellow or orange bell pepper, cored and chopped
1 large cucumber, peeled and chopped
¼ cup red onion, chopped
½ teaspoon dried dill

2 tablespoons balsamic vinegar
2 tablespoons Bragg Liquid Aminos
¼ teaspoon black pepper

1. In a mixing bowl, combine all ingredients and toss.
2. Refrigerate for at least two hours for best flavor.
3. Store refrigerated in a sealed container up to five days.
4. For a delicious addition, try adding a tablespoon of toasted sesame seeds.

Serves 2

Serving size: 2 cups

Nutrition Analysis per Serving: 60 calories, 0 grams fat, 2 grams protein, 14 grams carbohydrates, 3 grams fiber, 540 milligrams sodium

Other Noteworthy Nutrients per Serving (DV = Daily Value):

Vitamin C	— 270% DV	Iron	— 15% DV
Vitamin A	— 90% DV	Potassium	— 10% DV
Magnesium	— 15% DV		

Soy Sauce
Alternative

Nutritional Yeast

Nutritional yeast is a tasty product you can find in natural foods markets. These yellow flakes are a pure strain of yeast called *Saccharomyces cerevisiae* and, in the same family as edible mushrooms, have been used in food and beverage production for more than 5,000 years. Today, the same strain is used to brew beer, make wine, and leaven breads as well as develop the nutritionally-rich food called nutritional yeast.*

Each batch of nutritional yeast is grown on a mixture of cane and beet molasses for a period of seven days. B-vitamins are added during the process to provide the yeast with the nutrients it needs to grow. When harvested, the yeast is washed, pasteurized, and dried on roller drum dryers before it is ready for market. It is then used by food manufacturers in food products, added to boost the nutrient levels in pet foods, and simply packaged as is to be sold in natural foods stores.

Red Star® is the leading producer of this product, providing almost all of the nutritional yeast sold in the bulk section of natural foods markets. Vegans (strict vegetarians) have used it for years as a source of vitamin B_{12}, an essential nutrient found primarily in animal products. I use nutritional yeast because it tastes really good with certain foods (see below) and adds extra nutrients to my diet.

About Red Star®

Red Star is a division of the Lesaffre Yeast Corporation®, the largest manufacturer of yeast products in North America and has more than 50 years experience in the development and production of nutritional yeast products.

Unlike active baking yeast, nutritional yeast is grown solely for its nutritional value. It should not be confused with brewer's yeast, a by-product

Important Note: Nutritional yeast DOES NOT contain active yeast. It is generally considered acceptable in moderate amounts for those following a diet designed to manage *Candida albicans*.

of breweries and distilleries. Nutritional yeast is a low-fat, low-sodium, kosher, non-GMO food that contains no added sugars nor preservatives. The cane and beet molasses used in the growing process does not make nutritional yeast sweet and is not a source of simple sugars. For more information on Red Star, visit http://www.lesaffreyeastcorp.com/

NUTRITIONAL BENEFITS

After Red Star harvests its nutritional yeast, the company adds B-vitamins to replenish those lost during the washing process, making this yeast a remarkable source of these particular nutrients (see chart below). It provides an impressive amount of *complete* protein* per serving, as well as fiber, selenium, zinc, and other trace nutrients.

INGREDIENTS OF RED STAR NUTRITIONAL YEAST:

Inactive dry yeast, vitamin B_3, vitamin B_1, vitamin B_2, vitamin B_6, and vitamin B_{12}

Nutrients	Red Star Nutritional Yeast (1½ heaping tablespoons)
Calories	60
Total Fat	1 gram
Carbohydrate	7 grams
Fiber	4 grams
Protein	8 grams
Sodium	5 milligrams
Vitamin B_1 (thiamin)	640% Daily Value (DV)
Vitamin B_2 (riboflavin)	560% DV
Vitamin B_3 (niacin)	280% DV
Vitamin B_6	480% DV
Folic Acid	60% DV
Vitamin B_{12}	130% DV
Selenium	30% DV
Zinc	20% DV

* Only a handful of non-animal foods contain levels of amino acids high enough to be considered a complete protein. These include soy products, quinoa, amaranth, spirulina, and chlorella.

Two more beneficial compounds found in nutritional yeast are *beta-glucan* and *glutathione*. Beta glucans are non-digestible complex sugars found in oats, barley, nutritional yeast, algae, and mushrooms. Interestingly, research shows that beta glucans favorably support the immune system by activating *macrophages* and stimulating the release of protective *cytokines*. Macrophages are white blood cells that destroy microorganisms and remove dead cells. Cytokines are proteins that help regulate the immune system. In addition, beta glucans possess antioxidant and tumor-inhibitory properties.

Glutathione is a protein that plays a primary role in the body's detoxification processes. With the mineral selenium, glutathione forms the antioxidant complex *glutathione peroxidase* which protects cells against *free-radical* damage. Researchers agree that free radical damage occurs in most disease processes. Called the master antioxidant, glutathione peroxidase likely will be established as an anti-cancer agent. Nutritional yeast provides a remarkable 40 milligrams of glutathione per 1½ tablespoon serving. This is as much as found in an entire California avocado (a food commonly cited as an excellent glutathione source). To complete the antioxidant package, a serving of nutritional yeast provides 30% of the daily value of selenium.

Red Star nutritional yeast also provides 20% of the daily value of zinc per serving. Zinc is a key mineral that acts as a catalyst for 100 different enzymes. It is involved directly in DNA, RNA, and protein synthesis as well as being important for immune function, wound healing, physical growth and development, taste, smell, thyroid hormone function, and insulin action.

How to Use

Nutritional yeast has a slight cheese-like taste. It enhances the flavor of soups, salads, casseroles, sauces, salad dressings, gravies, baked potatoes, pasta, popcorn, and toast. Nutritional yeast can be purchased in a 4-ounce shaker container or as flakes or powder in the bulk section of most natural food stores (and is less expensive). Keep it stored in a cool, dark, dry place.

Nutritional yeast is a great addition to the diet. If you've never tried nutritional yeast, start by adding it to salads and on pasta. A favorite movie theater of mine in Eugene, Oregon offers nutritional yeast to add to your popcorn. If you like cashews and have a blender, try the Cashew Goddess Dressing recipe below tonight!

Hippie Wisdom

Cashew Goddess Dressing

⅔ cup roasted cashews
⅔ cup water
¼ cup lemon juice
3 tablespoons Red Star
nutritional yeast

2 tablespoons Bragg Liquid Aminos
½ teaspoon basil, dried
½ teaspoon fresh garlic, minced
¼ teaspoon dill, dried (optional)

1. Blend all ingredients in a food processor or blender until smooth. Add water for desired consistency.
2. Store in sealed container for 2–3 days. Enjoy!

Serves 12

Serving Size: 2 tablespoons

Nutrition Analysis per Serving: 50 calories, 3.5 grams fat, 0.5 grams saturated fat, 2 grams monounsaturated fat, 0.5 grams polyunsaturated fat, 2 grams protein, 3 grams carbohydrates, 0 grams fiber, 135 milligrams sodium

Other Noteworthy Nutrients per Serving (DV = Daily Value):

Vitamin B_1	—100% DV	Vitamin B_{12}	— 20% DV
Vitamin B_2	— 90% DV	Folate	— 8% DV
Vitamin B_6	— 80% DV	Magnesium	— 5% DV
Vitamin B_3	— 45% DV	Vitamin C	— 4% DV

Flaxseed Oil

Flaxseed oil is recognized today as having beneficial medicinal qualities. It is the single greatest plant source of an essential fat called *alpha-linolenic acid (ALA)*. ALA is a short-chain omega–3 fat in the same family as the long-chain omega–3 fats found in fish (see Section Three: *Fats & Oils*). Omega–3s, when consumed as part of the diet or as a supplement, reduce inflammatory markers in the body, thin the blood, improve insulin sensitivity, lower blood pressure, and offer numerous other health benefits.

Flaxseed oil is one of the best-selling products in the natural foods market today, but it is highly unlikely that you will find quality flaxseed oil in supermarkets anytime soon. The manufacturing and delivery process, both delicate and labor-intensive, makes flax oil more expensive and better suited to the natural foods market. A leading flax oil producer, Barlean's® takes the extra steps required to deliver the healthiest product possible.

> ## DID YOU KNOW?
>
> Hippocrates, the father of modern medicine, purportedly used flaxseed to relieve intestinal discomfort as far back as 650 B.C. The settlers of America used flaxseed for cloth fiber, and until World War I, a highly refined flaxseed oil (called linseed oil), was the primary oil used in paints and varnishes.

About Barlean's®

Dave and Barbara Barlean ran a fishing enterprise in 1972 before moving into flax oil production. It is rather remarkable that the Barleans moved to selling flaxseed from selling fish, these being, by far, the two primary sources of omega-3 fats in the diet as well as industries that place extra emphasis on freshness.

It turns out that Dave's son, Bruce, actually got the ball rolling in 1989, when he finished a job as a press operator for an organic oil producer. Bruce told Dave and Barbara that traditional flax oil was being pressed in such a crude way that excessive temperatures damaged the beneficial fats in the flaxseed. The taste was often rancid, and the oil needed filtering to make it palatable. The Barleans became intrigued with the idea of quality production, and before long they were selling flax oil on a wholesale level, using advanced pressing technologies to produce the purest oil possible. The Barlean's label was introduced in local stores in 1992, and since that time, sales of this organic, 100% unrefined, unfiltered flax oil have grown steadily to supply the national market.

The mechanical extraction method that Barlean's uses to press flaxseed oil preserves the natural flavor and quality of the seed itself. It also retains a greater concentration of the plant compounds called *lignans*. Lignans are a type of phytoestrogen that may protect against chronic diseases, such as hormone-dependent cancers, heart disease, and osteoporosis (see below).

Barlean's flax oil is third-party certified organic (see Section Three: *Organic Farming*) and is distributed directly to retail health food stores. The company takes great care to minimize the damaging effects of light, heat, and oxygen by packaging their flax oil in opaque containers and using refrigeration throughout the distribution. Barlean's insists that natural food markets replace their inventory of flax oil with fresh product if not sold within a four-month period. It is this kind of care and consideration that makes this an impressive and unique company. For more information on Barlean's, visit http://www.barleans.com/

NUTRITIONAL BENEFITS

Oily fish and fish oils are concentrated sources of healthy omega–3 fats. The primary fats of interest are *long-chain* fats, notably eicosapentanoic acid (EPA) and docosahexanoic acid (DHA). Studies show that 10% of *short-chain* alpha-linolenic acid (ALA) found in flaxseed oil is elongated to EPA whereas only 2%–5% is further lengthened into DHA.[56] Both of these longer chain omega–3 fats are associated with a host of health benefits including reduced heart disease risk. While fish is a better source of EPA and DHA, keep in mind that quality flaxseed oil has numerous compounds, including lignans, that are not found in any fish products.

Flaxseed Oil

In addition to the rich omega–3 content, flaxseed contains *one hundred* times more lignans than any other food. Research is underway to determine whether lignans can reduce heart disease risk and osteoporosis, relieve menopausal hot flashes, and slow the development and progression of kidney disease. When consumed, lignans are converted by beneficial bacteria in the colon to compounds that circulate to the liver. Researchers believe that lignans are estrogen modulators, balancing estrogen activity by exerting both weak estrogenic and anti-estrogenic properties. Experimental studies have demonstrated that lignans found in flaxseed exert anti-cancer effects.

Evidence suggests that elevated levels of inflammatory markers, such as *cytokines* and *C-reactive protein* (CRP), are linked to an increased risk for heart disease, rheumatoid arthritis, and other chronic diseases. You can reduce these inflammatory markers in your body if you consume flax oil on a regular basis. In one study, the equivalent of 1½ tablespoons of flax oil every day for four weeks reduced the inflammatory cytokines *interleukin–1 beta* and *tumor necrosis factor-alpha* by 30%.[57] In another study, fifty Greek men with elevated cholesterol levels took one tablespoon of flaxseed oil each day while another group of twenty-six men took one tablespoon of safflower oil. After three months, the men ingesting flaxseed oil had a 38% lower CRP level than the men consuming safflower oil.[58]

HOW TO USE

Look for high-lignan flax oil in the refrigerated sections in natural food stores or in capsule form in the supplement section. As a general goal, add one tablespoon to your diet each day. You will be treating yourself to approximately eight grams of ALA, the short-chain omega–3 fat.

Use flaxseed oil straight from the refrigerator or at room temperature since it is so delicate that heating can break down the essential fats into unhealthy by-products. You may find that flaxseed oil is an acquired taste. Try it straight from the spoon as a medicinal, create flax oil salad dressings (see recipe page 147), use it on baked potatoes, on toast, in smoothies, stirred into oatmeal, mixed into yogurt, or added to popcorn after popping. Remember to keep this oil refrigerated, and discard it after the expiration date, or if the flavor changes.

Quality flaxseed oil is a real health tonic, so buy a bottle and give it a try. If you hesitate to indulge in a bottle of oil, consider going the less expensive route: ground flaxseed. Your health will likely improve by adding flax oil or flaxseed into your diet. When buying flaxseed oil, look for:

Hippie Wisdom

- A reputable producer,
- Flax oil that is refrigerated,
- Flax oil that is packaged in a dark container,
- Production and expiration dates that are clearly marked on the container, and
- High-lignan flax oil made with organic, expeller-pressed flaxseeds.

Far Out! Flax Oil Dressing

½ cup Barlean's Organic Lignan Flaxseed Oil
¼ cup lemon juice
1 teaspoon Dijon mustard
1 clove garlic, minced

½ teaspoon oregano, dried
½ teaspoon basil, dried
½ teaspoon salt
Dash of black pepper

1. Put all ingredients into a jar with a tight-fitting lid.
2. Shake vigorously.
3. Store in refrigerator for up to one week.

Serves 6

Serving Size: 2 tablespoons

Nutrition Analysis per Serving: 160 calories, 18 grams fat, 1.5 grams saturated fat, 3 grams monounsaturated fat, 12.5 grams polyunsaturated fat, 0 grams protein, 1 gram carbohydrates, 0 grams fiber, 210 milligrams sodium

Other Noteworthy Nutrients per Serving (DV = Daily Value):
Omega 3s (ALA) — 10 grams

Miso

A Japanese creation, miso is a thick, rich, salty paste made from soybeans, grains, salt and a mold culture that has been aged in cedar vats for up to two years. There are more than forty varieties of miso, distinguished from one another by the type of grain and length of fermentation. Light or yellow-white miso typically is fermented from one to four months, red miso around eighteen months, and dark miso is fermented the longest, often as long as two years.

> **DID YOU KNOW?**
>
> Legend has it that miso was a gift from the gods to humanity as a way to ensure health, longevity, and happiness.

The traditional handcrafting of miso in Japan is virtually extinct; it has been replaced by large-scale computerized operations. Fortunately, the American Miso Company®, which is now the world's largest producer of traditional miso under the brand name Miso Master®, has preserved the ancient trade using wooden barrels imported from Japan.

About American Miso Company®

From 1979–1980, the founders of the American Miso Company studied under Takamichi Onozaki, a traditional miso maker in Japan. After learning the art, they built a production facility in Rutherfordton, North Carolina and invited Mr. Onozaki to the plant in 1981 to help the newly-established and ambitious company perfect its operations. Apparently all went well, for a full twenty-four years later the American Miso Company is producing eight varieties of miso. They use only organic, non-GMO (see Section Three: *Genetically Engineered Foods*) ingredients grown without chemical fertilizers, pesticides, herbicides, or fungicides, and none of the ingredients used in production have been irradiated, extracted with chemical solvents, or processed using artificial ingredients. All of the miso products under the Miso Master label are unpasteurized* to preserve the healthy bacteria produced during the fermentation process. For additional information on American Miso Company, visit http://www.great-eastern-sun.com/

Miso Master® Organic Miso

Variety	Aging Process
Organic Sweet White Miso (lower sodium)	1 to 2 months
Organic Chickpea Miso (soy-free)	1 to 3 months
Organic Corn Miso	2 to 4 months
Organic Mellow White Miso	2 to 4 months
Organic Mellow Barley Miso	2 to 4 months
Organic Traditional Red Miso	1½ years
Organic Brown Rice Miso	2 years
Organic Country Barley Miso	2 years

HOW MISO MASTER MISO IS MADE

Miso Master is gently aged and naturally fermented in huge cypress vats without added enzyme extracts.

Step One

Rinsed barley or rice is soaked and inoculated with *aspergillus oryzae* spores. The mixture is allowed to incubate for two nights. *Koji*, a mold impregnated grain, forms during this period. Koji provides the enzymes needed to digest the soybeans during the fermentation process.

Step Two

The koji is then mixed with the crushed soybeans and sea salt and placed into huge wooden vats in a temperature-controlled environment. Wooden planks covered with stones press the mixture as it ages, and after time, a dark fluid called tamari separates out. Tamari is the salty

*There are numerous health benefits from eating naturally fermented, *unpasteurized* foods. However, in certain cases, such as with tempeh, pasteurization is necessary to prevent the food from becoming *too* fermented when packaged for market.

liquid similar to soy sauce. The fermentation process of miso continues for up to two years before it is packaged and sold.

INGREDIENTS OF MISO MASTER ORGANIC BROWN RICE MISO:

> Organic soybeans, organic rice koji, sun-dried sea salt, well water, koji spores

NUTRITIONAL BENEFITS

There is strong evidence that eating fermented foods such as yogurt, sauerkraut, and miso has a positive impact on your health. These "living" foods have been shown to improve the digestibility and absorption of nutrients from the digestive tract. Beneficial cultures found in fermented foods support intestinal health by displacing unhealthy bacteria. When good bacteria thrives in the colon, the environment becomes more acidic (lower pH) which inhibits the growth of disease-causing bacteria.

While miso is nutrient dense, it is consumed in such small quantities that the vitamin and mineral contribution is relatively small. It is, however, an excellent source of the isoflavone *genistein*. Isoflavones (see Section Three: *Soy Products)* are plant-based estrogens that may exert beneficial effects in the body. Animal research and laboratory testing have shown that genistein inhibits breast, colon, and prostate cancer cells. The fermentation process significantly increases the concentration of genistein in miso as a result of the action of microbes that convert the isoflavone *genistin* into genistein.[59] In practical terms, two teaspoons of Miso Master Organic Brown Rice Miso provides almost 50% more genistein than a 4-ounce serving of tofu.

Studies show that the consumption of long-fermented miso, such as Miso Master Organic Brown Rice Miso, inhibits the progression of stomach,[60] colon,[61] and lung cancers[62] in animals. A study of nearly 22,000 Japanese women found that eating three bowls of miso soup daily as part of the regular diet reduced breast cancer risk by 40%. Two bowls of miso soup reduced cancer risk by 26%.[63] In the same study, those who consumed 25 milligrams of isoflavones each day had less than half the risk of developing breast cancer compared to those consuming only seven milligrams. Americans consume less than seven milligrams of iso-flavones a day on average.

NUTRITIONAL CAVEATS

I do have a concern about the sodium content of miso. While the amount of sodium in two teaspoons is not significant in the context of a healthy, low-sodium diet, greater intake of miso each day is a different story. Compare the different sodium levels below.

Miso Master Miso Brands	Sodium (per 2 teaspoons)
Organic Sweet White Miso	270 milligrams
Organic Chickpea Miso (soy-free)	340 milligrams
Organic Mellow White Miso	360 milligrams
Organic Corn Miso	390 milligrams
Organic Country Barley Miso	450 milligrams
Organic Traditional Red Miso	480 milligrams
Organic Brown Rice Miso	510 milligrams
Organic Mellow Barley Miso	520 milligrams

HOW TO USE

Use traditional miso varieties—such as barley, brown rice, and red miso—in bean dishes, stews, and soups. Try the lighter miso varieties, such as mellow barley, mellow white, chickpea, and sweet white miso, in cream-based soups or in dips, sauces, marinades, and salad dressings. You may find that a drizzle of flax oil on a piece of toast topped by a thin layer of mellow barley miso is a tasty snack. Miso will keep refrigerated in a closed container for at least three months.

Experiment with the many varieties of miso if you haven't already. Try a teaspoon in a cup of hot water with some freshly chopped scallions as a nourishing snack. Follow directions and use small amounts until you become more familiar with the flavor. Look for miso products that are:
- Made using organic, non-GMO soybeans, and
- Made without any preservatives.

Hippie Wisdom

Mystic Miso Soup

2 cups water
1 medium carrot, diced
1 celery stalk, diced
1–2 mushrooms, diced
¼ medium onion, chopped

1 clove garlic, minced
1 small piece ginger, minced
1 tablespoon Miso Master
  Organic Mellow Barley,
  Traditional Barley, or Red Miso

1. Bring all ingredients to a boil EXCEPT miso.

2. Cook for 2–3 minutes and remove from heat.

3. Mix 1 tablespoon of miso into soup. Do not add miso while water is still being heated because excessive heat will destroy the living cultures.

Serves 1

Nutrition Analysis per Serving: 80 calories, 1.5 grams fat, 0 grams saturated fat, 0.5 grams monounsaturated fat, 1 gram polyunsaturated fat, 4 grams protein, 16 grams carbohydrates, 4 grams fiber, 670 milligrams sodium

Other Noteworthy Nutrients per Serving (DV = Daily Value):

Vitamin A — 340% DV
Vitamin C — 15% DV
Potassium — 10% DV

Dulse (A Sea Vegetable)

Sea vegetables have been a part of the Japanese diet for thousands of years. Closer to home, they were traditionally used by Native Americans and early Irish and Scottish settlers in the Maritime Provinces of Canada. Today, many Americans are learning that sea vegetables are an incredible source of nutrients. As is the case with other vegetables, *seaweed* (as it is often called), contains other chemicals that will be proven beneficial in the future. There are only a handful of companies that harvest these plants in the United States. One of the leading producers of sustainably-raised sea vegetables is the Maine Coast Sea Vegetables® Company.

About Maine Coast Sea Vegetables®

Maine Coast Sea Vegetables was started in 1971 in a small town—you guessed it—on the coast of Maine. The company has grown steadily to provide Americans and Canadians with more than 30 tons of whole native sea vegetables harvested every year from the cold waters of the northern Gulf of Maine. It gathers four varieties of sea vegetables—dulse, kelp, laver (nori), and alaria (wakame)—by hand. Next, the vegetables are dried and graded for quality and certified organic by the OCIA (Organic Crop Improvement Association). Careful steps are taken, in accordance with organic guidelines, to ensure that the sea vegetables are sustainably harvested.

Maine Coast Sea Vegetables has worked to establish tighter standards within a largely unregulated industry. Environmental contamination is a major health concern regarding sea vegetables. The need for routine testing was recently demonstrated by a published study of seaweed products on the market. Fifteen different samples were taken from British Columbia, Japan, and Norway. Elevated levels of mercury, lead, arsenic, cesium–137, and radium–226 were found among the products tested.[64] Each year, Maine Coast Sea Vegetables tests to ensure that all of their seaweed products are free from these environmental pollutants and more. The tests check for 42 possible environmental contaminants, including herbicides, pesticides, hydrocarbons, and PCBs (polychlorinated biphenyls) as well as heavy metals such as arsenic, cadmium, lead, and mercury. A microbiology lab ensures that the dried seaweed products do not contain bacterial contaminants, including *E.coli*, yeasts, coliform, and harmful molds. For more information on Maine Coast Sea Vegetables and dulse, visit http://www.seaveg.com/

Dulse Flakes

Dulse (*Palmaria palmata*) is a popular sea vegetable that is unique to the North Atlantic and the Pacific Northwest. It is reddish in color and has a strong distinctive flavor and a soft, chewy texture. One of the products that Maine Coast Sea Vegetables sells is Dulse Flakes, the result of the dulse leaves having been cleaned, sun-dried, and chopped. It is ready to use straight from the package.

NUTRITIONAL BENEFITS

Calorie for calorie, dulse and other sea vegetables are the best source of nutrients. Specifically, dulse is an excellent source of vitamins, minerals, fiber, and living enzymes. A single serving of Dulse Flakes (one table-spoon) provides the following:

Nutrients	Maine Coast Sea Vegetables Dulse Flakes 1 tablespoon
Calories	13
Iodine	170% Daily Value (DV)
Vitamin B6	30% DV
Vitamin B12	15% DV
Iron	14% DV
Potassium	391 mg (10% DV)
Fiber	2 grams
Chromium	6% DV
Magnesium	5% DV
Sodium	87 milligrams

Dulse

Researchers are discovering the importance of potassium intake to help offset the blood pressure elevating effects of sodium. The ratio of potassium to sodium in dulse, at 4.5 to 1, makes it a great seasoning even for those with hypertension.

Dulse is a rich source of iodine, a mineral that plays an important role in healthy thyroid function. Iodine deficiency is the world's leading cause of mild to moderate brain damage. Nearly 50 million people worldwide experience some degree of brain damage resulting from an inadequate iodine intake. Iodine deficiency is also a direct cause of the thyroid condition called *goiter*. The increased number of salt iodization programs around the world has significantly reduced the incidence of these diseases.

One teaspoon of iodized salt contains 268 micrograms of iodine, or nearly double the recommended daily value. For a few decades after the salt fortification program began, thyroid conditions caused by *excessive* iodine became a real concern. But the pendulum has swung back the other way and recent changes in the food industry have reduced iodine levels in dairy products and in breads. In a survey conducted from 1988–1994, roughly 15% of women of child-bearing age were estimated to be deficient in iodine.[65] Compare the sources of dietary iodine below:

> **DID YOU KNOW?**
>
> To minimize the risk of disease caused by iodine deficiency, salt manufacturers started adding it to table salt in the United States in the 1920s.

Food	Iodine Content (micrograms)
Iodized salt (1 teaspoon)	268
Dulse Flakes (1 tablespoon)	260
Centrum* multivitamin (1 tablet)	150 (100% DV)
Seafood (3.5 ounces)	20–116
Turkey (3.5 ounces)	40

* Centrum is a registered trademark of Wyeth

While thyroid problems can be caused by too little or too much iodine in the diet, a benefit of keeping iodine intake at the upper normal range is protection against the effects of radiation. While we hope this is not a health risk that we will face, it is worth noting. The use of iodine pills or natural sources of iodine such as sea vegetables have long been recommended as a way to saturate the thyroid with a healthy form of iodine (iodine–127). This simple step prevents the absorption of any radioactive iodine (iodine–131) that results from nuclear fallout and which is known to cause thyroid problems and cancer.

Authorities recommend 80–150 micrograms of iodine each day, although research shows that up to 1000 micrograms per day is probably safe for the majority of the population.[66] Individuals with thyroid conditions should consult their healthcare practitioner if they have questions regarding iodine intake. Dulse is a better source of iodine than salt because it also contains other beneficial nutrients.

Iodine and/or iodine-rich seaweeds may prevent breast and stomach cancer. Japanese women have significantly lower rates of breast cancer than American women and some researchers hypothesize that seaweed may lower both the incidence of benign and malignant breast disease.[67] In animal studies, the seaweed *wakame* suppressed breast tumor growth[68] and another seaweed commonly eaten in Japan, *mekabu*, inhibited breast cancer progression in three types of human breast cancer cells in laboratory experiments.[69]

HOW TO USE

I recommend experimenting with sea vegetables, which you may find to be an acquired taste if you're unfamiliar with Asian cooking. Try a well-prepared seaweed salad available in Asian restaurants and specialty markets. Dulse Flakes and other sea vegetables can be included in your diet in many different ways, such as:

- Added to salads and allowed to sit a few minutes to tenderize before serving.
- Added to soups such as minestrone, chowder, and bouillabaisse. Use ¼ cup to start and add more as desired. Less salt will be needed in the soup recipe.

- Added to stir fry dishes a couple of minutes before serving. Less salt or soy sauce will be needed.

Sea vegetables are a great way to add some flavor and nutrients into your diet. Try ordering seaweed salad the next time you see it on a menu. At the natural foods market, look for high-quality sea vegetables that are:
- Tested for environmental contaminants, and are
- Harvested sustainably.

Hippie Wisdom

Check It Out! Corn Chowder

1 tablespoon extra-virgin olive oil

1 medium yellow onion, chopped

1 cup water

1 small to medium red potato (4–6 ounces), chopped into ½-inch pieces

1 cup organic corn

1 cup chopped broccoli

2 cups Almond Breeze Original almond milk

½ teaspoon salt

1 heaping tablespoon Maine Coast Sea Vegetables dulse flakes

¼ teaspoon black pepper

1. Heat olive oil over medium-high heat in large pot.

2. Add onion and sauté for 2–3 minutes or until tender.

3. Add water and potatoes. Turn heat to high, bring to boil, and cook for 7–8 minutes.

4. Add corn, broccoli, soymilk or almond milk, and salt. Cook for 3–4 minutes at medium-high heat.

5. Add dulse flakes and pepper. Cook for 1–2 minutes and serve.

Serves 2

Serving Size: 2 cups

Nutrition Analysis per Serving: 240 calories, 8 grams fat, 1 grams saturated fat, 6 grams monounsaturated fat, 1 gram polyunsaturated fat, 7 grams protein, 42 grams carbohydrates, 6 grams fiber, 650 milligrams sodium

Other Noteworthy Nutrients per Serving (DV = Daily Value):

Vitamin C	— 100% DV		Vitamin A	— 25% DV
Iodine	— 90% DV		Potassium	— 25% DV
Vitamin E	— 50% DV		Folic Acid	— 15% DV
Calcium	— 25% DV		Magnesium	— 10% DV
Vitamin D	— 25% DV		Iron	— 10% DV

A Closer Look at the Main Issues

The natural foods market strives to offer foods that are as *wholesome* as possible. To the contrary, an ordinary supermarket makes few claims about how their food products are produced and are more focused on keeping costs low than delivering the healthiest foods possible. There are many controversial issues that stem from the use of technological "advances" embraced by large food producers. This section briefly discusses a few of the main issues, including the risks of chemicals used to produce food, the unknowns associated with genetic engineering, and the concerns regarding preservatives. This section also discusses the role of specific foods in the diet.

Antibiotics

Hormones

Environmental Chemicals

Genetically Engineered Foods

Organic Farming

Food Additives

Milk Products

Wheat Products

Soy Products

Fats & Oils

Antibiotics

The Centers for Disease Control and Prevention (CDC) estimates that foodborne diseases cause nearly 80 million illnesses and 5,000 deaths annually in the United States.[70] Beef, pork, poultry, and fish have been found to be the cause of more than half of these disease outbreaks, based on follow-up reports conducted by the CDC.

Scientists agree that bacteria are becoming more and more resistant, due in part to their increased exposure to antibiotics, making specific antibiotics no longer effective against certain pathogens. The American Medical Association and the World Health Organization have requested that the agriculture industry stop using the same antibiotics in livestock that are also used to treat sickness in people.

Antibiotics are used in agriculture in four different ways: disease prevention, disease treatment, disease control, and growth promotion.[71] Efforts to reduce antibiotic use are aimed at those used for growth promotion and disease prevention. The European Union voted to ban the use of antibiotics to promote growth in livestock in 1998 while here at home, at least fifteen percent of antibiotics used are for growth promotion. One of these growth enhancers is an antibiotic called *virginiamycin*. Since the agriculture industry began regularly using this medication, a foodborne pathogen (disease-causing bacteria) called *enterococci* has developed resistance to the antibiotics given to people to treat this illness.

The issue of antibiotics speaks to a larger problem—*intensive farming*. Crowding and stress promote disease conditions. It is easy to imagine that a few sick chickens can jeopardize the health of thousands of other birds sharing the same environment. As a general rule, farmers act quickly to stop the spread of disease by using effective antibiotics. Enrofloxacin (Baytril®) is one of two such antibiotics known as fluoro-quinolones that were approved by the FDA for use in poultry in 1995. The other was sarafloxacin (Saraflox®).

The antibiotic equivalent of Baytril® used in humans is Cipro®. Prior to 1995, it was effective in treating people who were sick from a bacterial illness called *Campylobacter* (usually contracted by eating contaminated meat) that afflicts two million people in the U.S. every year. As a result of frequent exposure to Baytril®, however, *Campylobacter* has become resistant to Cipro®. The CDC estimates that nearly 1 in 5 cases of foodborne illness caused by *Campylobacter* is now fluoroquinolone resistant, and officials expect this resistance to increase.

The FDA proposed a ban on these two antibiotics in October 2000, and Abbott Laboratories® quickly removed Saraflox® from the market, but Bayer®—the manufacturer of Baytril®—has fought the proposed ban. Today the largest poultry producers (Tyson®, Perdue Farms®, and Foster Farms®) are no longer using Baytril® preventatively, but they still are using it to treat diseased chickens.

It seems clear that, in the long run, supporting farmers that raise antibiotic-free animals will help reform current agricultural practices. For more information, visit the Center for Science in the Public Interest webpage on antibiotics at http://www.cspinet.org/ar/

Hormones

The natural foods market offers different animal products labeled *hormone-free*. What does this actually mean?

There are two types of hormones used in animal agriculture: *protein* hormones and *steroid* hormones. Protein hormones must be administered by injection because when fed orally, the hormone is degraded by digestive enzymes. Steroid hormones can be administered by injection, time-release implants, or as an additive to feed.

There are six different steroid hormones currently approved by the FDA for use in food production in the United States. They are:

- **Estradiol**: natural female sex hormone
- **Progesterone**: natural female sex hormone
- **Testosterone**: natural male sex hormone
- **Zeranol**: synthetic growth promoter
- **Trenbolone acetate**: synthetic growth promoter
- **Melengestrol acetate**: synthetic growth promoter

Currently, the FDA allows the use of all of these hormones in cattle and sheep but NOT in chickens, turkeys, ducks, or pigs.[72] The primary concerns regarding steroid hormone usage in animal agriculture are potential reproductive problems and cancer risk in both animals and humans. Many people recall the problems caused by a synthetic form of estrogen called DES. Widely used on cattle and chickens in the 1950s, DES was later found to cause vaginal cancer in humans and was withdrawn from the market in the late 1970s. No conclusive evidence indicts today's steroid hormones since there exist no long-term safety studies comparing regular exposure with populations eating animal foods free of hormones. Until more is known, it is wise to avoid any potential health risks associated with steroid hormones.

Unlike steroid hormones, protein hormones *normally* are broken down in our digestive tract when we consume them. One protein hormone in the midst of controversy is called bovine growth hormone (BGH). It was approved for use in dairy cattle (not in beef cattle) in 1993. Monsanto®, the manufacturer of BGH, introduced this hormone as a way to boost the milk production of dairy cows. Critics express three main concerns about using BGH: elevated levels of a hormone called insulin-like growth factor (IGF–1) in milk; the increased reliance on antibiotics to treat cows given BGH; and the unhealthy feedstuff that is used to meet the increased energy demands of the cow given BGH.

IGF–1, a powerful hormone secreted by the liver, plays a key role in wound healing and maintaining healthy bone structure. IGF–1 is touted in some circles as an anti-aging remedy. It appears, however, that IGF–1 is a double-edged sword. The scientific evidence suggests that elevated plasma levels of IGF–1 increase cancer risk, notably breast, prostate, and colon cancers. Studies show that IGF–1 production increases in the body when a person consumes more calories, protein, and milk.[73] Now add to the equation the undisputed evidence that cows treated with BGH produce milk containing 70% higher levels of IGF–1. Most scientists maintain that when this milk is consumed, the IGF–1 proteins are digested into harmless amino acids and are not absorbed into our bodies as active IGF–1. Perhaps this is the case in a healthy digestive tract. However, some individuals suffer from intestinal permeability, also called *leaky gut syndrome*. Damage to the intestinal lining caused by medications, food allergies, non-steroidal anti-inflammatory medications (NSAIDS), and stress enable protein molecules to enter the bloodstream intact. These proteins can trigger an immune response. While the prevalence of leaky gut syndrome is not known, most individuals with Crohn's disease and 10% to 20% of their healthy relatives suffer from this condition.[74] The *only way* to avoid the potential risk associated with elevated IGF–1 levels in cow's milk is to choose organic milk.

Many consumers remain wary of BGH and point to other potential health concerns. After eight years of review, Canada rejected BGH use in dairy production based partly on the fact that BGH increases the prevalence of an infection in dairy cows' udders called *mastitis*. Antibiotics are the standard treatment for mastitis, so an increased risk of mastitis means a higher reliance on antibiotics. It is not surprising then, that tests have shown that antibiotic residues occur in milk samples. While the

Food and Drug Administration (FDA) has established "safe levels" and "tolerance levels" of antibiotics in milk, the concerns shared by many are whether these added chemicals are, in fact, acceptable when natural and healthy alternatives are readily available.

Finally, increased production of milk, in addition to increasing the overall stress on the cow, requires more energy-dense feed. In the U.S., rendered protein and industry byproducts, including poultry waste, are regularly used to meet these energy needs. The industry aggressively recycles rendered protein and *waste* products, which can lead to problems as described in an article published in the LA Times on January 4, 2004: *"When feed containing rendered cattle is given to poultry, some of it scatters on the floor as the birds peck at it. The floor is also thick with excrement, feathers, dirt and bits of straw. Rather than throw all that waste away, farmers sweep it up and recycle it—by selling it as cattle feed. The FDA allows that practice, which is common in the big chicken-producing states of the Southeast."*[75]

Fearing the spread of mad cow disease in the U.S., the FDA imposed a partial ban on feeding rendered cow proteins back to cattle in 1997. Exempted from this ban, however, is the use of rendered swine, chickens, horses, blood, milk, and gelatin as animal feed. The industry estimates that more than 47 billion pounds of animal by-products are transformed into feed as well as industrial materials.[76]

It is disturbing that the livestock industry routinely feeds animals and waste products back to the animals to speed the growth process and ultimately save money. It is clear that feeding animal products to cows (whose natural diet is exclusively vegetarian) including *cow* by-products, will create health problems for us and that it is an unethical and unwise practice. No wonder consumers are seeking out organic meat and milk products with increasing interest. Organically raised animals are not given antibiotics, growth hormones, or feed that contains ANY animal byproducts and by purchasing these foods, you are effectively changing agricultural practices with your dollar.

To find out more about BGH and to stay up-to-date on important information about your family's food safety, visit the website of the Organic Consumers Association (OCA) at www.organicconsumers.org

for a free bi-weekly news brief. The OCA is a grassroots non-profit public interest organization established in 1998 that deals with crucial issues of food safety, industrial agriculture, genetic engineering, corporate accountability, and environmental sustainability. The OCA represents more than 500,000 members, subscribers, and volunteers as well as hundreds of companies in the natural foods and products marketplace.

Environmental Chemicals

Eating the fat of animals—in foods such as butter, red meat, ice cream, cheese, and whole-milk dairy products—is the greatest source of chemical exposure for most Americans. These chemicals (also called *persistent organic pollutants* by scientists) originate from manufacturing industries, incinerators, and from agricultural use and include pesticides such as *dieldrin* and *DDT,* industrial chemicals like *hexachlorobenzene,* and the broad class of *dioxins.* All of these linger in the environment for decades and accumulate in the fat stores of animals and humans. Among other potential health concerns, there is evidence that these chemicals raise cancer and diabetes risk.

The U.S. Environmental Protection Agency (EPA) estimates that 90% of dioxin exposure comes directly from animal fats. Once ingested, dioxin can enter the nucleus of a cell and damage DNA. Foods that have the highest dioxin concentrations are dairy products, meat and poultry, eggs, fish, and animal fats such as butter and lard.[77]

The EPA released a report in 2000 estimating—as a worst case scenario—that cancer risk from dioxin exposure, independent of other sources, is one in 100, or ten times the prior estimate made in 1994.[78] Certain man-made chemicals, including some of the dioxins, are called endocrine disrupters and may alter reproduction in a wide range of animals, including humans. Dioxin levels in animal fats are difficult to reduce. Crops become contaminated by airborne dioxins, primarily from incinerators. Dairy cows and beef cattle absorb this class of toxins when feeding on contaminated crops. The most effective way to reduce dioxin is to reduce your consumption of animal fats.

While choosing organic animal products cannot protect you from dioxin exposure, it will reduce your overall exposure to other environmental contaminants. Animals treated with antibiotics or hormones or fed grains grown with pesticides and herbicides have fat stores that contain higher chemical levels than those raised organically and fed organic feed.

Genetically Engineered Foods

A serious controversy is stirring over the use of *genetically engineered foods*. You may want to research this contentious topic more on your own. For now, a good start might be to recognize the terms commonly used to refer to biogenetic engineering: they are GMO (or "genetically modified organism"); GE (or "genetically engineered"); or just GM ("genetically modified.")

Biogenetic engineering, henceforth called GMO, is the process of splicing (combining) one or more genes of a plant or animal into another plant with the hope of creating beneficial properties for the new plant and for consumers. Today, more than 75% of the soybean crop planted is a GMO crop called Roundup Ready®. These soybeans contain a gene derived from a microorganism that makes soybeans resistant to the herbicide Roundup® made by Monsanto®. The herbicide can then be sprayed directly on soybean crops, effectively killing the weeds without killing any of the soybean plants and without purportedly causing any ill effects to the soybeans themselves. Approximately 40% of the current U.S. corn crop is a Roundup Ready crop or has been modified to contain a gene taken from bacteria that produces a protein with insecticidal properties. Other GMO crops currently being grown are cotton, canola, and potato, while varieties of oats, rice, grapes, and others are still in development.

Advocates of genetic engineering believe that there is great potential for the newly designed crops. For example, GMO rice contains higher levels of vitamin A. Using this rice in developing countries could greatly reduce the incidence of blindness caused by vitamin A deficiency. Closer to home, the arguments for GMO foods is that they will allow farmers to use *fewer* pesticides to manage pests.

Concerned scientists and researchers, however, express grave caution related to the unknown havoc that such tinkering with our food supply might have on human health and the environment. There is so much that we *do not know* about the potential risks of these crops. Could a GMO crop, for instance, produce a toxin or other chemical in any creature eating it? Could GMO foods trigger serious allergic reactions? Could insects develop a greater resistance to current pesticides and non-chemical methods used by organic farmers, thus causing disease and crop failures? Could *beneficial* insects be harmed by eating GMO crops? Could GMO crops create "super-weeds"? These are serious unanswered questions that need to be addressed to our satisfaction before proceeding forward.

Only long-term safety testing will supply the answers—until then it is a grand experiment with potentially disastrous effects. Unlike other potential health risks, such as hormones in animal production, the GMO issue can quickly spread out of control. You already are unwittingly consuming GMO crops, such as corn and soybeans, as ingredients in some of your favorite foods. There are currently no special labeling laws designating the presence of GMO foods. When GMO crops are grown on a larger scale, foods containing their ingredients will become increasingly more difficult to track and avoid. You will not have the choice to avoid GMO ingredients when dining out in most restaurants or any other time that you eat away from home. Consumer advocacy groups are demanding the labeling of all GMO foods to ensure that you have the right to make a choice in this matter.

Many natural foods producers go to great lengths to ensure that no GMO ingredients are in the foods they produce. Look for the non-GMO label (indicated voluntarily) on many of the natural foods that you currently use. Continue to keep abreast of this developing issue by visiting the Organic Consumers Association (www.organicconsumers. org) or the Center for Food Safety (CFS). CFS was established by the International Center for Technology Assessment in 1998 to address the impacts of our food production system on human health, animal welfare, and the environment. CFS works to achieve its goals through grassroots campaigns, public education, media outreach, and litigation. For more information, visit http://www.centerforfoodsafety.org/

Organic Farming

The United States Department of Agriculture (USDA) established a national standard to define organically produced foods in 2001. In simple terms, organic food is produced without irradiation, the use of sewage sludge, genetically modified organisms (GMO), most conventional pesticides, or the aid of synthetic fertilizers. The regulations also prohibit antibiotics and hormone use in organic meat and poultry, and meats labeled as organic must be fed 100% organic feed. The complete definition established by the USDA is more than 500 pages long and can be viewed in its entirety at www.ams.usda.gov/nop/

Before a product can use the *USDA Organic* seal, a government-approved certifier (also called a third-party certifier) inspects both the farm where the food is grown and the growing process to ensure that the USDA organic standards have been met. Any further processing of the organic food before it reaches the supermarket or restaurant is also subject to inspection. Look on the label for more information on the certifying party. For example, one of the leading third-party certifiers is Quality Assurance International (QAI).

By law, there are four different labeling references that indicate the percentage of organic ingredients contained in a product by weight (only food products that contain 95–100% certified organic ingredients are permitted to use the USDA Organic seal):

1. 100% Organic Ingredients
2. 95–100% Organic Ingredients
3. 70–95% Organic Ingredients
4. Less than 70% Organic Ingredients

For many farmers, organic growing encompasses more than just the issue of fertilizers and pesticides. They also place emphasis on using renewable resources, conserving soil and water, taking better care of farm animals, and maintaining the environment for future generations.

For more information, visit the Organic Consumers Association (www. organicconsumers.org).

For years, people have questioned whether organic food is more *nutritious* than conventionally produced food. A recently published study found that organically produced foods do contain higher levels of certain nutrients. In a review of 41 different studies and 1,240 food comparisons, organic crops were found to contain significantly more vitamin C, iron, magnesium, and phosphorus as well as fewer nitrates than conventional crops.[79]

Prioritizing Organic Food

My clients often ask me what organically grown foods they should buy if they had to prioritize. Without hesitation, I tell them to choose organic foods that are highest on the food chain—meats, milk, eggs, yogurt, cheese, ice cream, and cottage cheese. After animal products, I recommend that they select certain fruits and vegetables to buy organically. It makes sense when prioritizing to avoid the fruits and vegetables known to have higher levels of pesticide residues.

Thanks to a grant from Stonyfield Farm® and the efforts of the Environmental Working Group (EWG), we now have a complete *Shopper's Guide to Pesticides in Produce*. The guide (see page 171) ranks pesticide contamination for 47 popular fruits and vegetables based on an analysis of more than 100,000 tests that were conducted by the USDA from 1992–2001. Pesticide residues were measured in six different ways, after which a composite score was determined and assigned to each crop.

The EWG estimates that a person can lower his or her pesticide exposure by *90 percent* by replacing the top twelve most contaminated fruits and vegetables with the least contaminated. Of the top twelve containing the greatest pesticide contamination, eight are fruits: peaches, strawberries, apples, nectarines, pears, cherries, red raspberries, and imported grapes. The four vegetables that make the top twelve list are: spinach, celery, potatoes, and sweet bell peppers.

Of the twelve least contaminated fruits and vegetables, seven are vegetables. These are: sweet corn, avocado, cauliflower, asparagus, onions, peas, and broccoli. (Choose organic corn to avoid varieties that have been genetically engineered.) The five fruits rounding out the least contaminated category are pineapples, mangoes, bananas, kiwi, and papaya.

Harmful effects from pesticides—as demonstrated in animal studies—include cancer, nervous system damage, and reproductive irregularities. Pesticides are more damaging to a developing fetus and are more toxic to all of us when we are exposed to multiple contaminants. EWG recommends washing produce, peeling vegetables, and buying organic whenever possible. The complete list is provided below. For additional information, see http://www.foodnews.org/

Shopper's Guide to Pesticides in Produce

(The crop with the highest pesticide contamination is assigned a score of 100)

Rank	Food	Combined Score
1	Peaches	100
2	Strawberries	89
3	Apples	88
4	Spinach	85
5	Nectarines	85
6	Celery	83
7	Pears	80
8	Cherries	76
9	Potatoes	67
10	Sweet Bell Peppers	66
11	Raspberries	66
12	Grapes—Imported	64
13	Carrots	57
14	Green Beans	57
15	Hot Peppers	55
16	Oranges	53
17	Apricots	51
18	Cucumbers	51

Rank	Food	Combined Score
19	Tomatoes	48
20	Collard Greens	48
21	Grapes—Domestic	47
22	Turnip Greens	41
23	Honeydew Melons	40
24	Lettuce	40
25	Kale	39
26	Mushrooms	36
27	Cantaloupe	36
28	Sweet Potatoes	35
29	Grapefruit	34
30	Winter Squash	34
31	Blueberries	30
32	Watermelon	27
33	Plums	26
34	Tangerines	25
35	Cabbage	25
36	Papaya	23
37	Kiwi	23
38	Bananas	19
39	Broccoli	18
40	Onions	17
41	Asparagus	16
42	Sweet Peas	13
43	Mango	12
44	Cauliflower	10
45	Pineapples	6
46	Avocado	4
47	Sweet Corn*	1

* Author's note: Approximately 40% of all corn planted in the United States today is genetically modified (see Section Three: *Genetically Engineered Foods*).

Food Additives

Have you noticed that reading the ingredient list on food products can be really difficult? You might think I am talking about the small print on the package; however, I am referring to the lengthy chemical terms interspersed between recognizable foods like wheat, honey, and yeast. Consider the ingredients in this supermarket bread product:

> Enriched wheat flour, water, high fructose corn syrup, whole-wheat flour, yeast, wheat bran, soybean oil, brown sugar, ethoxylated mono and diglycerides, mono and diglycerides, salt, wheat gluten, soy lecithin, calcium sulfate, potassium bromate, sodium stearoyl lactylate, calcium dioxide, calcium iodate, alpha amylase, molasses, soy flour, vinegar, datem, soy fiber, triticale, rye meal, oats, cornmeal, cracked wheat, monocalcium phosphate, flaxseed hulls, ammonium sulfate, calcium carbonate, vinegar, calcium proprionate

Most authorities view these additives without concern, but some of these chemicals simply are unhealthy. As for the rest, well, there really is no way of knowing for sure. Aside from natural antioxidants like vitamin E, the purpose of these additives is not to improve your health; they are used for shelf-life and profit margin only. The question arises: In this day and age of airtight packaging, refrigerated trucks, daily deliveries, product on demand, and warehouse-sized freezers, why do we need *any* preservatives?

Why do we accept synthetic chemicals in our food? We have so much to learn about the potential effects of additives in relationship to auto-immune diseases, chronic fatigue syndrome, fibromyalgia, learning disabilities, and cancer. Why take the risk? Recent history has provided many examples which exposed the population to certain chemicals, believing them safe, only to learn otherwise. American soldiers were instructed to dust themselves with DDT in World War II to prevent lice. In the 1970s, dieldrin, which has been shown to double breast cancer risk, was sprayed on apples. As recently as the 1980s, municipal incinerators discharged more than 600 times more dioxin into the air than is permitted today. We know now that dioxin is linked to cancer and diabetes risk and look back at these situations in disbelief of our ignorance.

You and I can choose to challenge the common assumption that it is perfectly fine to consume a steady diet high in additives. Some of the preservatives currently found in foods are clearly deleterious to our health. Below are recommendations for evaluating additives developed by the Center for Science in the Public Interest.[80]

EVERYONE SHOULD AVOID
(These are unsafe in the amounts consumed or are very poorly tested.)

Acesulfame K
Artificial Colorings: Blue 1, Blue 2, Green 3, Red 3, Yellow 6
Olestra
Potassium Bromate
Saccharin
Sodium Nitrate, Sodium Nitrite

CERTAIN PEOPLE SHOULD AVOID
(These cause allergic or other reactions in some people.)

Artificial Colorings: Yellow 5
Artificial and Natural Flavoring
Aspartame
Caffeine
Cochineal or Carmine
Gums (Tragacanth)
Hydrolyzed Vegetable Protein
MSG (Monosodium Glutamate)
Quinine
Sulfites (Sodium Bisulfite, Sulfur Dioxide)

CAUTION
(These may pose a risk and need to be better tested)

Artificial Colorings: Citrus Red 2, Red 40
Aspartame

Brominated Vegetable Oil (BVO)
Butylated Hydroxyanisole (BHA)
Butylated Hydroxytoluene (BHT)
Heptyl Paraben
Propyl Gallate
Quinine

CUT BACK

(These are not toxic, but large amounts may be unsafe or unhealthy.)

Caffeine
Corn Syrup
Dextrose (Corn Sugar, Glucose)
High Fructose Corn Syrup (HFCS)
Invert Sugar
Mannitol
Partially Hydrogenated Vegetable Oil
Salatrim
Salt
Sorbitol
Sugar (Sucrose)

SAFE

(These appear to be safe, though a few people may be allergic to any single additive.)

Alginate
Alpha Tocopherol (Vitamin E)
Ascorbic Acid (Vitamin C)
Beta-Carotene
Calcium Proprionate
Calcium Stearoyl Lactylate
Carrageenan*
Casein
Citric Acid
EDTA

---

* Author's Note: While carrageenan is listed as safe, this thickener is under investigation for potential health risks. Many natural food manufacturers do not use carrageenan or are seeking a suitable replacement.

Erythorbic Acid
Ferrous Gluconate
Fumaric Acid
Gelatin
Glycerin (Glycerol)
Gums (Arabic, Furcelleran, Ghatti, Guar, Karaya, Locust Bean, Xanthan)
Lactic Acid
Lactose
Lecithin
Modified Starch
Mono- and Diglycerides
Phosphates, Phosphoric Acid
Polysorbate 60, 65, 80
Potassium Sorbate
Propylene Glycol Alginate
Sodium Ascorbate
Sodium Benzoate
Sodium Carboxymethylcellulose (CMC)
Sodium Caseinate
Sodium Citrate
Sodium Propionate
Sodium Stearoyl Fumarate
Sodium Stearoyl Lactylate
Sorbic Acid
Sorbitan Monostearate
Starch
Sucralose
Thiamine Mononitrate
Vanillin, Ethyl Vanillin

Milk Products

Milk has strong advocates and harsh critics. On one hand, milk is by far the leading source of calcium in the American diet. In addition to contributing to a healthy bone structure, more dietary calcium may lower your risk of colon cancer. Research has shown that a person with hypertension can lower his or her blood pressure by adding low-fat dairy products to a healthy diet.[81] On the other hand, *whole-milk* dairy products are the main source of saturated fats in the diet. Higher-fat milk products are also the source of harmful pesticides and environmental chemicals. Finally, milk products are not well-tolerated by everyone, as we will review.

Despite the United States Department of Agriculture (USDA) food guide pyramid recommendation, there is no "one-size-fits-all" guideline for milk products; you need to make your own decision. Do you experience health problems that may be worsened by milk products in your diet? Do you notice any adverse physical symptoms after consuming milk products? If you feel well after consuming milk products, then I recommend that you choose organic, low-fat dairy products. Even if you don't have doubts about the role of milk products in your diet, I suggest that you read on.

Over the years, the USDA and the National Dairy Council have promoted the idea that cow's milk is a requirement for all of us. The main selling point has been the role of calcium-rich milk in the development and maintenance of healthy bones. While calcium *is* an essential mineral, there are food sources other than milk that provide calcium. The majority of the world's inhabitants, including Asians, consume very little or no milk products. Studies show that these cultures actually have *lower* bone fracture rates than Americans. How is this possible?

Bone metabolism is complex: the key players include exercise and nutrients such as vitamin K, magnesium, folate, phosphorus, sodium, and protein. This complexity explains why milk consumption or calcium intake is not always protective against osteoporosis. As evidenced by

Asian populations, it is possible to meet the daily calcium needs without any milk products by regularly choosing calcium-rich foods (see below).

Non-Dairy Food Sources of Calcium

Food	Calcium* (milligrams)
Collards (1 cup cooked)	360
Soy milk, enriched (1 cup)	300
Firm tofu, ½ cup (with calcium)	258
Dried figs (5)	258
Turnip greens (1 cup cooked)	250
Sardines, canned (2 ounces)	220
Blackstrap molasses (1 tablespoon)	187
Kale (1 cup cooked)	180
Broccoli (1 cup cooked)	178
Bok choy (1 cup cooked)	158
Mustard greens (1 cup cooked)	150
Navy beans (1 cup)	128
Tahini (2 Tbsp.)	128
Great northern beans (1 cup)	121
Almond butter (2 Tbsp.)	86
Orange (1 medium)	56
Cabbage (1 cup cooked)	50
Romaine, green, red leaf lettuce (1 cup raw)	38

*The Daily Value for calcium is 1000 milligrams. One cup of cow's milk contains 300 milligrams of calcium.

Lactose Intolerance, Milk Allergies, and Milk Intolerance

Lactose intolerance is one reason that so many people world-wide do not use milk products. For genetic reasons, some individuals do not produce *lactase*, the enzyme needed to digest the milk sugar lactose. Researchers estimate that 100% of Native Americans, 80% of Blacks (world-wide) and Latinos, and 15% of persons with northern European descent are unable to break down lactose.[82] Beyond lactose intolerance, a person could have an *allergy* to milk, or as is the case most often, exhibit *sensitivities* to milk products.

Milk (including cheese, butter, yogurt, and ice cream) is one of the top eight allergenic foods. These top allergenic foods, which include wheat, soy, eggs, peanuts, tree nuts, shellfish and fish, cause 90% of all food allergies. Cow's milk contains more than 25 different proteins that are the potential source of an allergy or sensitivity. The primary proteins responsible for reactions are *B-lactoglobulin, casein (alpha-, beta-,* and *kappa-), alpha-lactalbumin,* and *bovine serum albumin.* Reactions in the body to milk proteins that involve the immune system (mainly IgE-mediated reactions) are considered a *cow's milk protein allergy.* Cow's milk protein sensitivity appears to involve the IgG-mediated portion of the immune system.

The incidence of cow's milk protein allergy and protein sensitivity during *infancy* in western industrialized countries has been estimated to be only about 2–3%.[83] Cow's milk protein allergy disappears or greatly improves for many infants as they grow into childhood.[84] Sensitivity to specific milk proteins, however, is more likely to persist into adulthood, possibly contributing to a host of disease conditions.

Diagnosing lactose intolerance begins by paying better attention to any physical symptoms—such as gassiness, cramping, and diarrhea—that occur after consuming milk or other milk products. If you suspect lactose intolerance, try lactose-free milk or use lactase tablets with milk products. Do the symptoms disappear? If you are still uncertain, your physician can schedule a *hydrogen breath test* that measures the hydrogen content of your breath after drinking a lactose-containing beverage. High levels of hydrogen indicate lactose intolerance. Choosing lactose-free milk and milk products that contain less lactose—like yogurt—are two ways to still consume dairy products without suffering ill effects.

It is more difficult to diagnose a milk allergy or milk sensitivity. Symptoms that occur during or shortly after eating milk products are useful for proper diagnosis. Allergies or milk sensitivity may cause excessive mucus production, irritable bowel symptoms, congestion, runny nose, skin irritations such as rashes, hives or eczema, asthma, or general feelings of tiredness.

In addition to noticing symptoms, there are two diagnostic methods commonly used by allergists (allergy specialist doctors) to assess food sensitivity or allergy. The first is the *skin prick test* which is the least expensive method. It entails pricking the skin on your back or forearm with an extract of an allergen of the food or substance in question. A doctor can evaluate specific reactions within 15-20 minutes. A second common diagnostic tool is called *RAST* (*Radioallergosorbent test*). It requires extracting a blood sample and sending it to a laboratory where antibodies are measured and results are typically available within one week.

Treating a milk allergy or sensitivity is more challenging than managing lactose intolerance. The only solution is to avoid or significantly reduce all milk products. More physicians are recommending that patients with certain conditions, such as persistent allergies, chronic respiratory conditions, frequent colds, bronchitis, sinus conditions, and autoimmune diseases avoid all milk products for a significant period of time. This approach—called an *elimination diet*—is the most effective way to treat food intolerance.

If you suspect a cow's milk sensitivity, I recommend that you eliminate *all* milk products for *at least* a month. In some instances, several months may be necessary to experience improved health. After this time period, I suggest that you re-introduce milk products several times in the same day— called a *food challenge*—to provoke a potential reaction. Both the elimination diet and the food challenge will help you determine if milk products are the source of health problems.

To eliminate the wide variety of milk products and foods containing milk proteins requires diligence. In addition to the obvious dairy foods, like butter, cheese, milk, ice cream, yogurt, sour cream, and cottage cheese, milk-based ingredients are found in dozens of other common foods. The following ingredients contain dairy products: milk solids, whey, nonfat dry milk, casein or caseinate, lactose, lactalbumin, galactose, and hydrolyzed protein (may contain casein). The definition of "non-dairy" on the label technically allows the presence of up to a half of one percent of milk by weight. If you choose to remove all milk products from your diet and feel overwhelmed by the task, consult with a registered dietitian or experienced nutritionist to help you plan your menu.

Wheat Products

Wheat is the basis for nearly all of the bread products and pastas we consume. Yet, we rarely eat wheat in its whole form, as *wheat berries*, or bake using whole-wheat flour. Today's widespread consumption of wheat and, in particular, refined wheat flour products has introduced certain disease risks. These concerns, along with questions regarding wheat sensitivity, necessitate some discussion of the role of wheat in your diet.

Flour mills grind wheat berries into three distinct parts: the *bran*, the *germ*, and the *endosperm*. Millers remove the wheat germ and the wheat bran and sell them separately, most often as feed to livestock. White flour is the remaining fraction that is packaged and sold to supermarkets, commercial bakeries, and food manufacturers.

Surveys indicate that white bread is the preference among most Americans. White flour and products made with white flour became widely popular in the early 20th century. Doctors soon began noticing a sharp increase in nutrient deficiency diseases that were caused by this dietary shift. In 1942, Congress passed the Enrichment Act requiring processors to supplement white flour with some nutrients that had been lost by removing the bran and germ, namely: vitamin B_1 (thiamin), vitamin B_2 (riboflavin), vitamin B_3 (niacin), and the mineral iron. In 1998, the vitamin folate was also added to the required nutrient list. While these additives addressed the more immediate deficiency worries, they did not rectify the loss of the majority of other nutrients. The difference between whole-wheat and white flour remains profound. Compared to white flour, whole-wheat flour contains:

1800% more vitamin E	400% more fiber
800% more vitamin B_6	300% more potassium
600% more magnesium	200% more calcium
500% more manganese	200% more copper
400% more zinc	

And these are only some of the nutrient differences. The refining process strips away a long list of beneficial plant chemicals found in the bran and the germ.

The average American gets 20%–30% of his or her daily calories from white flour products. The nutrients NOT available in this flour have a profound negative impact on the quality of the diet. Remember, specific nutrients in whole-wheat have been shown to lower the risk of heart disease, cancer, diabetes, and stroke. For example, researchers have discovered that *magnesium* found in whole-wheat is essential for proper carbohydrate metabolism and that a deficiency of magnesium is linked to diabetes. Another whole-wheat flour nutrient, fiber, slows the absorption of dietary sugars, maintains intestinal regularity, reduces cholesterol levels, and probably lowers the risk of colon cancer. Research will continue to find health benefits associated with the *hundreds* of different plant chemicals found in the wheat berry. Adding more whole-wheat into the diet lowers disease risk and is recommended for all who do not have wheat allergies or gluten sensitivities.

Wheat Concerns

Inspite of all that wheat has to offer, it is one of the leading allergenic foods. Anthropologists agree that, historically, wheat is a recent addition to the diet. For the last two million years, humans were hunter-gatherers and did not regularly consume grain foods. A few thousand years ago, wide-spread agriculture made wheat one of the mainstay foods in the diet. Today, we expose ourselves to wheat many times a day when we eat breakfast cereals, biscuits, bagels, pancakes, waffles, sandwich bread, pita bread, French bread, crackers, tortillas, pizza, pasta, pretzels, cakes, cookies, and pastries. Frequent exposure to a single food can increase your sensitivity to that food, even to the extent of *creating* an allergic reaction. However, true wheat allergies are rare, and while many people believe they are allergic to wheat, most are mistaken. It is more likely that they suffer from the more common gluten sensitivity.

Gluten Sensitivity

Some researchers believe that some degree of gluten sensitivity may be present in up to 30% of the population, with symptoms varying widely. Some experience noticeable reactions such as diarrhea or rashes after eating wheat. Others do not. Antibody testing can reveal the presence of gluten sensitivity where no symptoms are discernible. High-powered electron microscopy—used in research settings—has shown signs of intestinal inflammation caused by gluten sensitivity that typically would be missed using routine diagnostic measures.[85] It is unclear whether the gluten sensitive individual will develop the clinical features of celiac disease (true wheat allergy) over time. You may improve gluten sensitivity noticeably by sharply reducing your intake of all wheat and gluten-containing foods for several weeks. Significant differences, however, may not occur unless *all* gluten is removed from the diet for three to six months before being re-introduced.

Wheat Allergy (Celiac Disease)

A true wheat allergy, known as *celiac disease* (also called gluten sensitive enteropathy), is believed to affect less than 1% of the population. The disease results from an immunological reaction, within the inner lining of the small intestine, to a mixture of two proteins in wheat—*gliadin* and *glutenin*—together called *gluten*. In addition to all wheat products, gluten is found in spelt, kamut, rye, barley, and, to a lesser extent, oats.

The symptoms of celiac disease can range from a few mild signs to severe symptoms, such as chronic diarrhea, excessive gas and distension, unexplained iron deficiency anemia, rashes, weight loss, and more serious disease conditions. Some researchers think that the prevalence of celiac disease is much higher in American than currently believed.[86] Diagnoses can be tested by conducting blood antibody tests and a small intestinal biopsy.

The blood tests designed to detect celiac disease measure *endomysial antibodies, anti-tissue transglutaminase antibodies*, and *antigliadin antibodies*. An individual with elevated endomysial and anti-tissue transglutaminase antibodies has more than a 95% chance of having celiac. Anti-gliadin antibodies have a much higher false positive rate because there is an immunologic hyper-reactivity leading to gluten sensitivity. If you suspect celiac disease or gluten sensitivity, consult with an allergist who can order the appropriate blood tests and intestinal biopsy where necessary.

I encourage everyone—whether gluten sensitivity is suspected or not—to replace some of the wheat in the diet by choosing spelt and different whole grains avoid over-exposure to wheat and reap the benefits of a varied diet.

Following a gluten-free diet is a *must*, however, for those with celiac disease (which means no spelt flour). There are gluten-free breads and pasta products on the market made from rice flour, quinoa, and other grains with no gluten. Individuals with celiac can likely tolerate amaranth, corn, millet, quinoa, teff, and wild rice. Find a registered dietitian or experienced nutritionist for help in planning a diet that is completely gluten-free.

Soy Products

Soy products have been embraced by hippies for several decades and Asian cultures for centuries. More recently, there has been steady growth and general acceptance of a variety of soy products in the mainstream diet. The potential health benefits of adding soy to the diet have sparked much of this interest. Not everyone is on board with soy, however; there are some that are allergic or sensitive to soy and others that are outspoken critics. This section briefly explores these issues and the current recommendations.

The soybean is very unique. It has nutritional characteristics resembling a hybrid of regular beans and nuts. Soybeans have far more fat (albiet a healthy fat) than any other bean and significantly more protein than any nut.

Percent of Calories from Fat, Protein and Carbohydrate

	Fat	Protein	Carbohydrate
Nuts	77%	14%	14%
Soybean	44%	36%	20%
Other Beans	4%	27%	72%

Since soybeans are a good source of high-quality protein (contains adequate levels of specific amino acids), soy-based foods are an excellent choice for vegetarians and those trying to reduce animal protein in their diet. There is ongoing extensive research underway to examine the possible benefits from eating soy products. Scientists initially became interested in soybeans after noticing dramatically lower rates of heart disease and certain cancers among Asian populations who eat soy regularly.

Soybeans & Health

Research has consistently shown that individuals with high cholesterol levels (greater than 250 mg/dl) can benefit from 2–4 servings of soy each day. More than 27 studies have been conducted to determine if soybean protein consumption can lower total cholesterol and reduce heart disease risk. The research has found that making no lifestyle changes other than replacing equal amounts of animal protein with 20–30 grams of *soy protein* daily (see page 188) can lower cholesterol approximately 10–15% over a period of 8–12 weeks. The FDA has approved the following label claim for products containing at least 6.25 grams of soy protein per serving: "Diets low in saturated fat and cholesterol that include 25 grams of soy protein a day may reduce the risk of heart disease."

Soybeans also contain plant-based estrogens known as *isoflavones*. These substances, particularly *genistein*, are being studied for their ability to reduce the cell growth-promoting effect of circulating estrogens made by the body which may reduce the risk of cancer. Animal studies show positive health benefits of genistein, and researchers are seeking to determine if similar effects occur in humans.

Soy Allergy and Soy Sensitivity

Like any food, soy is not for everyone. Soy is categorized as one of the top eight allergenic foods, and yet, actual allergies are rare. Less than 1% of all infants are truly allergic. Furthermore, the majority of soy allergies are outgrown by the time an infant reaches two years of age. Adults are more likely to experience a *soy sensitivity*.

There are at least fifteen specific proteins in soybeans that are responsible for allergic reactions. Symptoms include acne and other skin conditions, congestion, asthma, fatigue, weakness, nausea, diarrhea, gastrointestinal problems, itching, hay fever, hives, and anaphylaxis.

Individuals with soy sensitivity generally do well by avoiding soy milk, soy-based veggie burgers, tofu, and other soy products. If you suspect an allergy to soy, consult with an allergist. A registered dietitian or experienced nutritionist can help you identify allergies and plan menus that are completely free of all soy products.

Soy Concerns

Be aware that some authorities are very critical of soy products. Critics say that soy contains "anti-nutrients" such as *trypsin inhibitors* that can severely disrupt nutrient absorption. They further claim that soy contains *goitrogens* that interfere with thyroid function and that the isoflavones in soy disrupt your body's hormonal balance.

While raw soybeans do contain trypsin inhibitors, cooking greatly reduces their effect. Tests that Eden Foods® conducts, for example, show only a trace of trypsin inhibitors in their soymilk. "Anti-nutrients" may not be all bad, either; there is evidence that small amounts of anti-nutrients in soybeans such as *protease inhibitors* and *phytates* actually exert cancer preventative effects in the body.[87]

Goitrogens are substances found in a number of foods such as edamame (green soybeans), cabbage, cauliflower, turnips, peanuts, and broccoli. Goitrogens theoretically could pose a risk to thyroid function, occurring in individuals who eat large quantities of goitrogen-containing foods and have a low iodine intake. Researchers agree that a couple of servings of soy products each day does not provide a high level of goitrogens. If you do have concerns about thyroid function, consult with your physician for the appropriate tests.

Isoflavones exert very weak estrogenic effects. Researchers agree that when consumed at levels approximating two soy servings daily (50 milligrams isoflavones), the presence of isoflavones actually lowers the overall estrogenic effect in the body. Scientists are exploring this anti-estrogenic effect as a possible mechanism for lower cancer rates among those regularly consuming soy products. Until more is known about exactly how phytoestrogens work in the body, health experts recommend soy *foods* instead of concentrated soy supplements. Women with a family history of breast cancer are advised to add up to a couple of servings of soy each day. There remains some uncertainty regarding the effect of soy intake for those with breast cancer. For now, women with breast cancer are advised NOT to start adding soy into the diet until more is known.

How Much Soy?

While the definitive answer remains unclear, leading experts such as former National Cancer Institute researcher Dr. Mark Messina, suggest as much as two servings of soy on a daily basis. This amount—roughly 15 grams of soy protein and 50 milligrams of isoflavones—is an estimate of what people living in Asia have eaten for centuries. It is also a recommendation based on clinical findings, population studies, and safety data.

Protein and Isoflavone Content of Soy-Based Foods

Soy-Based Food	Serving Size	Soy Protein (grams)	Isoflavones (milligrams)
Texturized soy protein (dry)	¼ cup	6 grams	94 mg
Soy nuts (dry roasted)	¼ cup	10 grams	84 mg
Miso	2 teaspoons	1 gram	76 mg
Green soybeans (Edamame)	¼ cup	11 grams	70 mg
Tempeh	4 ounces	19 grams	60 mg
Soy flour	¼ cup	8 grams	44 mg
Tofu	4 ounces	13 grams	38 mg
Stonyfield Soy Yogurt	4 ounces	4 grams	26 mg
Soy milk	1 cup	4–10 grams	20 mg
Soy-based veggie burger	1 patty	12–18 grams	5–20 mg
Other soy meat analogues	1 ounce	4–10 grams	5–20 mg
Soy nut butter	2 tablespoons	8 grams	17 mg
Soy hotdog	1 hotdog	7–11 grams	5–10 mg
Soy Sauce, Soy Oil	—	0	0 mg

Soy products can be a great addition to the diet, particularly for those who are replacing higher fat animal foods. It is impossible to recommend any specific amount for every person. I encourage my clients to experiment by adding a few servings per week and noticing how the soy foods affect their health. Some say they do not feel well after consuming soy-based products. Others say they feel great!

All soy foods are not created equal. The range of choices include whole-food soy products and highly processed soy products. I recommend that you emphasize whole food soy products such as green soybeans (*edamame*) and the fermented soy products tempeh and miso in your diet. Slightly more-processed soy foods are tofu and soymilk. Even more-processed soy foods are veggie burgers and soy-based meats. While I recommend less processed soy foods, some folks improve the overall quality of their diet by replacing fast-food and high-fat animal products with veggie burgers. I do not recommend the regular use of fractionated soy products such as powders, soy isolates, and soy isoflavone supplements because of the potential adverse effect of concentrated phytoestrogens and the potential to induce soy sensitivity.

Fats & Oils

- Types of Fats
  - Saturated Fats
  - Trans Fats (Hydrogenated Oils)
  - Polyunsaturated Fats
  - Monounsaturated Fats
- Nuts & Seeds
- Oils

Types of Fats

Like most people, I am happy that we have made peace with healthier types of dietary fat. It is hard to believe that we ever recommended against plant fats such as almonds and avocados. Today we know better. Yet, there is still disagreement regarding the best fats and oils to eat. The more recent evidence and my own thoughts relating to saturated, trans fat, polyunsaturated fats, and monounsaturated fats, are discussed below.

Saturated Fats

American favorites such as beef, bacon, butter, cheese, and ice cream are the premier sources of saturated fat in the diet. A body of research has shown that higher intakes of saturated fat drive up total cholesterol and LDL cholesterol which are considered heart disease risk factors. Still, controversy abounds even with saturated fats.

It is essential to realize that saturated fat is not a detriment to your health when eaten in *moderation*; it is excess saturated fat that is the problem. Too much of it contributes to high cholesterol and an increased diabetes risk.

Most health authorities recommend a reduction in *overall* saturated fat intake to less than twenty grams of saturated fat daily (see chart on page 193). However, different *types* of saturated fats exert different effects in the body. In other words, researchers are no longer lumping saturated fat into a single category. Dietary studies are complicated by the fact that one food may contain a blend of different saturated fats, making it difficult to pinpoint their specific effect in the body. At present, the saturated fats ranked from having the worst effect on cholesterol levels to those having the least or no effect[88] are:

1. Myristic acid
2. Palmitic acid
3. Lauric acid
4. Stearic acid

These four saturated fats, which are distinguished by the number of *carbons* contained in their chemical structure, exhibit the following characteristics:

- **Myristic acid** (14-carbons): When added to the diet, myristic acid raises total cholesterol more significantly relative to the good cholesterol (HDL) than any other saturated fat. Primary sources of myristic acid are ice cream, cheese, butter, and lard; palm kernel and coconut oils.
- **Palmitic acid** (16-carbons): When added to the diet, palmitic acid raises cholesterol, but to a lesser extent than myristic acid. Primary sources are palm oil and animal fats including red meat and poultry.
- **Lauric acid** (12-carbons): When added to the diet, evidence shows that lauric acid raises blood cholesterol the most but also significantly raises the beneficial HDL cholesterol. This might mute the negative effects to some extent. Lauric acid converts to monolaurin, a compound that has antiviral and antibacterial properties.[89] Primary sources of lauric acid are coconut oil, palm kernel oil, and to a lesser degree, milk fat.
- **Stearic acid** (18-carbons): When added to the diet, stearic acid does not raise cholesterol. Primary sources are red meat and cocoa butter. That's right, chocolate lovers, cocoa butter!

In a typical American diet, the primary saturated fat consumed is palmitic acid, followed by stearic acid, myristic acid, and lauric acid. Japanese people, who have very low heart disease rates, eat a daily diet that contains on average only one gram of myristic acid. Americans consume six grams of myristic acid daily.

For years, most health authorities have regarded the tropical oils—coconut, palm kernel, and palm oil—as highly saturated fats to be avoided. Unfortunately, this research was based largely on tests using hydrogenated and highly-refined tropical oils. *Less-refined* tropical oils contain plant chemicals that make the oils healthier. For example, coconut oil may increase metabolism and provide antibacterial properties. Moderation with all oils is still the primary determinant of health.

Higher quality tropical oils are now available in natural foods markets. Let's take a closer look at them:

- **Coconut Oil**—75% saturated and 25% unsaturated. The saturated fats are 37% lauric, 16% myristic, 15% palmitic and 4% stearic acid.
- **Palm Kernel**—82% saturated and 18% unsaturated. The saturated fats are 45% lauric, 20% myristic, 10% palmitic and 1% stearic acid.
- **Palm Oil**—50% saturated and 50% unsaturated. The saturated fats are 1% lauric, 2% myristic, 38% palmitic acid and 5% stearic acid. Of the unsaturated fats in palm oil, 40% are oleic acid, the same monounsaturated fat in olive oil. Several studies have found that palm oil does not raise cholesterol levels.[90]

As you can see above, palm oil contains very little myristic acid and is largely unsaturated. Quality palm oil, which is a component of Earth Balance® (see food category: *Butter Alternative*), is becoming a more popular ingredient in natural food products.

While it is difficult to focus on any specific saturated fat, future recommendations may target foods containing higher amounts of myristic acid. A healthy goal is to consume less than twenty grams of total saturated fat (particularly those from animal sources) and less than three grams of myristic acid each day. As shown by the chart below, this goal is difficult when following a traditional American-style diet.

Total Saturated Fat and Myristic Acid Content of Common Foods

	Saturated Fat	Myristic Acid
Ice Cream (1 cup of regular vanilla)	14.8 grams	2.50 grams
McDonald's Quarter Pounder w/cheese	11.2 grams	1.50 grams
McDonald's Large French Fries	9.1 grams	0.50 grams
Hamburger (3.5 ounces—regular)	8.2 grams	0.50 grams
Butter (1 tablespoon)	7.5 grams	1.50 grams
Hotdog (1 regular beef-based)	6.9 grams	0.50 grams
Cheese (golf-ball size)	6.0 grams	1.00 gram
Biscuit	6.0 grams	0.25 grams
Whole Milk (1 cup)	5.6 grams	1.00 gram
Yogurt (1 cup of whole milk yogurt)	4.8 grams	0.80 grams
Bacon (3 pieces)	3.5 grams	0.25 grams

Trans Fats (Hydrogenated Oils)

Food manufacturers began wide-spread use of a process called hydrogenation in the 1950s with the goal of replacing butter with a solid spread made from liquid vegetable oil. The hydrogenation process changes the chemical structure of a fat—which changes its melting point—thereby transforming liquid corn oil into hard-stick margarine. Hydrogenated oils have a much longer shelf-life than liquid oils. All of this may sound good, but trans fats are not "native" species, meaning they are not recognized by the body. When eaten as a regular part of the diet they cause the malfunction of cellular processes. Evidence correlates trans fat intake with heart disease, diabetes, inflammatory diseases, and possibly cancer.

I strongly urge you to avoid foods containing hydrogenated or partially hydrogenated oils, such as hard-stick margarine, as much as possible. Commercially prepared foods are the primary source of trans fats today. They include: pastries, pie crusts, cookies, crackers, snack chips, french fries, fried chicken, and biscuits. Consider how often you eat these commercial produced foods and devise a plan to avoid or replace them. For example, one easy way to avoid trans fats is to buy healthier snack chips (see food category: *Tortilla Chips*).

Polyunsaturated Fats

Polyunsaturated fats are very important to include in a healthful diet. There are two *essential* fats, omega–6s and omega–3s, that our bodies must obtain from food (we cannot synthesize them from other fats). Omega–6 fats are abundantly available in vegetables and vegetable oils such as corn, safflower, sunflower, soybean, and "vegetable" oils. Omega–3 fats are found in flaxseed and oily fish (see chart below) and to a lesser degree in green leafy vegetables. The majority of Americans have an extremely low omega–3 fat intake whereas omega–6 intake is too high due to the consumption of commercially prepared foods. For example, soybean oil, which is mostly omega–6 fats, represents 80% of commercially used oils.

Researchers estimate that our natural diet thousands of years ago consisted of roughly four times more omega–6 fats then omega–3 fats, or a four to one ratio. Today, with vegetable oil intake skyrocketing, many of us are eating *twenty* times more omega–6 fats than omega–3 fats (20 to 1 ratio). Excessive omega–6 fat intake can stimulate the increased production of inflammatory compounds in the body that are linked to arthritis, heart disease, ulcerative colitis, and autoimmune diseases like lupus. The authors of one study that analyzed the inflammatory markers of more than 850 men and women in relation to omega–3 fat intake and omega–6 intake actually found no evidence that omega–6 fats *caused* detrimental effects. Their conclusion, however, cited that omega–6 fats are more likely to raise inflammatory markers for individuals with a *low level* of omega–3 fats in the diet.[91] Research has shown that increasing omega–3 fat intake from both flaxseed and fish lowers such inflammatory markers.[92]

I think that increasing omega–3 fats in the diet is particularly important for those who are still eating a diet high in animal fats and processed foods with fewer fruits, vegetables, and other whole foods. One easy way restore balance is by adding two to three servings of fish that contain the highest concentrations of omega–3 fats (see chart below).

Fish and Omega–3 Content (grams) per 3.5 ounce serving	
More than 1.0 gram	Anchovies, bluefish, herring, Spanish mackerel, king mackerel*, salmon, sardines, lake trout*, bluefin tuna*, albacore tuna*
0.5 grams—0.99 grams	Striped bass*, sea bass*, rainbow trout*, blue mussels, oysters, flounder, halibut*
Les than 0.5 grams	Carp, catfish, clams, crab, cod, grouper*, lobster*, perch, mahi mahi, mullet, orange roughy*, pike, red snapper*, scallops, sea trout*, shrimp, sole, squid, sturgeon, swordfish*, canned light tuna (not albacore)

*Caution: Fish with higher concentrations of mercury.

Another way to restore essential fat balance is to eat more omega–6 fats as plant foods (vegetables, some nuts, seeds, and tahini). Nature packages these foods with antioxidants and other valuable nutrients to help your body metabolize them more effectively. Start by adding the following foods into your diet on a regular basis (see below).

Food Sources of Omega–3 Fats and Omega–6 Fats					
	Short-Chain Omega 3s	Long-Chain Omega 3s	Total Omega 3s	Omega 6s	Omega 3 to Omega 6 Ratio	Calories
Flax oil (1 teaspoon)	2.7 grams	None	2.7 grams	0.6 grams	4.5 to 1	40
Wild Salmon (and other oily fish) (3.5 oz.)	0.3 grams	1.2 grams	1.5 grams	0.4 grams	4.3 to 1	150
Ground flaxseed (1 tablespoon)	1.6 grams	None	1.6 grams	0.4 grams	4 to 1	45
Kale (1 cup cooked)	0.13 grams	None	0.13 grams	0.10 grams	1.3 to 1	36
English Walnuts (1 ounce)	2.6 grams	None	2.6 grams	10.8 grams	1 to 4.2	185

Monounsaturated Fats

A study comparing the dietary patterns of Greek men with American men in the 1960s changed our understanding of fat.[93] At the time, Greek men were eating the same amount of total fat as American males but had only a fraction of the heart disease incidence. Since then, we've learned that the specific type of fats abundant in the traditional Greek diet, called *monounsaturated* fats, are healthier for the heart.

The primary sources of monounsaturated fats in a typical Greek diet include olives, nuts, seeds, avocados, and olive oil. The specific fatty acid in each of these foods, called *oleic acid*, is classified as an omega–9 fat. Such monounsaturated fats and oils are also a source of beneficial plant chemicals. Extra-virgin olive oil, for example, contains two powerful antioxidants, *oleuropein* and *hydroxytyrosol*. Researchers believe that in addition to oleic acid, olive oil is a superior choice because of these antioxidants.

Nuts and Seeds

It wasn't long ago that leading health authorities were recommending that we avoid eating nuts and seeds mainly due to their high fat content. Several recent studies have changed this thinking. Findings indicate that eating five servings of nuts, including peanuts, each week (one serving of almonds equals a small handful) can lower heart disease risk by 30%–50%.[94] They are a great source of heart-healthy monounsaturated fats, vitamin E, folic acid, copper, magnesium, arginine, and phytochemicals. Independently, these nutrients are known to play a beneficial role in maintaining cardiovascular health; in combination, they are even more protective.

Oils

Food markets today carry an unprecedented selection of oils. The impact of these oils on your health, however, depends on the type of oil you are choosing as well as the production method.

There are two possible extraction techniques: mechanical (expeller-pressing) or solvent extraction. Expeller-pressing extracts oils with a device that forces the crushed seeds against a metal head. The less-expensive solvent extraction method relies on chemical solvents, such as *hexane*, to separate the oil from the seed. Both methods produce oil that can be sold to natural food stores as *unrefined*. The majority of these, though, go on to be processed to a greater degree to generate refined oils which have a longer shelf-life and a higher smoke point (the temperature which causes the oil to degrade). These oils, labeled as *refined oils*, can be found at both natural food stores and supermarkets. Most of the oils found at supermarkets, however, have undergone *even further* refining including de-gumming, bleaching, and deodorizing to give them the longest shelf life possible.

Unrefined expeller-pressed oils retain more of the nutritive value than the more common solvent-extracted oils. The nutrients maintained in expeller-pressed oils, which include antioxidants, are needed to help your body metabolize the oil more efficiently. Natural food manufacturers regularly use *high-oleic* sunflower or *high-oleic* safflower oil—an oil from a plant variety that was hybridized (using traditional methods)— to replace some of the omega–6 fats with oleic acid, an omega–9 fat. Oleic acid, the primary fatty acid in olive oil, is metabolized very well by the body.

I recommend that my clients use *organic, expeller-pressed* oils whenever possible. These oils, which are made from seeds, nuts, or beans, are grown without the use of synthetic pesticides, fungicides, fertilizers, or herbicides. Spectrum Naturals® is a company that makes a wide-variety of quality products, including mayonnaise, made with expeller-pressed oils.

The healthiest type of oil to use daily is *extra-virgin* olive oil (organic is preferable). The phrase "extra-virgin" indicates that the oil was derived from the first pressing of the olive. A more refined—yet suitable oil—is *light* olive oil if it is produced by a trusted manufacturer. I also recommend small amounts of unrefined organic sesame oil; organic, expeller- or mechanically-pressed grapeseed oil; organic, expeller-pressed high-oleic safflower oil; and organic, expeller-pressed high-oleic sunflower oil. Two quality oils used to replace hydrogenated fats in many foods—organic coconut oil and organic palm oil—can be added to the diet in small amounts.

I suggest that you take steps to minimize the amount of rancid or damaged oils that you consume. Buy oil in smaller containers, keep it out of the light, and consume it within three months. You may wish to refrigerate your oils to prolong their shelf life, although olive oil solidifies at cooler temperatures and should be stored in a dark pantry. Avoid heating oils at high temperatures when possible. High temperatures damage fatty acids and create free radicals.

The degradation process accelerates when the oil begins to smoke. Take a moment to learn what oils to use when frying, sautéing, wok-frying, baking at high temperatures, and searing food, and choose an oil that has a high smoke point. As you notice from the chart that follows, refined oils have a much higher smoke point than unrefined oils and are the best choice when cooking at high temperatures. Mechanically-pressed grapeseed oil is a favorite among chefs because it is antioxidant rich and has a neutral taste. Other cooking oils recommended for higher temperatures include:

Cooking Oil	Smoke Point
Avocado (refined)	520 degrees
Almond (refined)	495 degrees
Grapeseed (refined)	485 degrees
Super canola* (refined)	450 degrees
Super high-oleic * safflower oil (refined)	450 degrees
High-oleic sunflower oil (refined)	450 degrees
Sesame (refined)	410 degrees

* Made by Spectrum Naturals®

Next, keep a selection of healthy oils ideal for medium or lower temperatures (no more than medium on your stovetop). Use these oils to lightly sauté vegetables, to prepare sauces, and to bake at low temperatures:

Cooking Oil	Smoke Point
Sesame (unrefined)	350 degrees
High-oleic safflower oil (unrefined)	320 degrees
High-oleic sunflower oil (unrefined)	320 degrees
Extra-virgin olive oil (unrefined)	250–325 degrees

A Word on Canola Oil

Canola oil has been at the center of controversy for the last decade. Most health professionals recommend canola oil because it contains 60% monounsaturated fats and 10% omega–3 fats (alpha-linolenic acid). It is commonly used to prepare foods that require a neutral tasting oil.

Canola oil comes from the rapeseed plant. Older varieties of the rapeseed plant contain *euricic acid*, a toxic fatty acid, and critics question the safety of today's canola oil suspecting that it still contains this harmful substance. There are myths being perpetuated on the internet—based on the toxicity issue—that blame numerous health problems on the use of canola oil. There is no evidence to support any of these claims.

The truth is that canola was developed in Canada in the 1970s through traditional plant breeding methods to remove the euricic acid content: Thus, canola oil on the market today averages less than 1% euricic acid (older varieties contained 30%–60%). There are brands of canola oil, however, that are healthier than others. Canola oil commonly sold in supermarkets is produced by extraction methods that use high temperatures and chemical solvents. A genetically engineered canola plant crop is currently being cultivated and will become the primary source of most of the canola oil on the market. For these reasons, I do not recommend any supermarket brands of canola oil. Spectrum Naturals makes several organic (non-GMO), expeller-pressed canola oil products that are available in natural foods markets. For more information, visit http://www.spectrumnaturals.com/truthcanola.html/

Epilogue

Thanks for taking the time to ponder what I've had to say in this volume of *A Yuppie's Guide to Hippie Food*—I hope it has inspired you to eat a healthier diet.

One of my main goals in writing this book (as well as future volumes) is to positively affect the food *choices* available to all of us. I'd like restaurants to offer antibiotic-free chicken, organic milk, and omega-3 rich eggs. When traveling, I'd like to be able to buy quality snack foods and drinks at regular convenience stores. I'd like to have the choice to eat more whole grains, bean dishes, and foods containing nuts and seeds when I'm away from home. While this may seem like wishful thinking, I believe that if we start asking for these options (and we are willing to pay for them), they will become available. I am reminded of the quote:

"Never doubt that a small group of thoughtful, committed citizens can change the world. Indeed, it's the only thing that ever has."

—Margaret Mead

I encourage you to view it as fun and challenge yourself to improve your diet this year. Start keeping track of all of the new foods that you try. Consider that buying healthy food not only provides your body with better nutrition but also reinforces the farmer or producer who cares enough to deliver a superior product to the market. Great possibility will arise from this way of thinking.

The recipes included in this book were created for those of you looking for dishes that are quick, healthy, and tasty. Let me know which ones you enjoy. If you have any questions or comments, email me at Greg@hippiefood.com.

I write a newsletter on the latest from the natural foods market called *Hippie Wisdom*. You can sign-up at www.hippiefood.com to receive your monthly copy. It's free.

I wish you well on your journey towards better health!

Peace,

Greg

COMING SOON:
The Best Natural Foods on the Market Today:
A Yuppie's Guide to Hippie Food,
Volume II

List of Recipes

Shopping List

CHICKEN	Bell & Evans, Eberly Poultry, MBA Poultry, Petaluma Poultry
EGGS	Cage Free DHA Omega-3 Eggs (Gold Circle Farms)
MILK	Organic Valley Low-fat Milk
SOY MILK	Edensoy Extra Original (Eden Foods)
ALMOND MILK	Almond Breeze Vanilla (Blue Diamond)
YOGURT	Stonyfield Farm
SOY YOGURT	WholeSoy
COTTAGE CHEESE	Horizon Organic Lowfat
BUTTER ALTERNATIVE	Earth Balance (GFA Brand)
BREAD	Sprouted Whole-Wheat Bread (Food for Life)
ALMOND BUTTER	Woodstock Farms
CEREAL	GrainShop Cereal (Barbara's Bakery)
JUICE	Just Concord Grape Juice, Organic Prune Juice (R.W. Knudsen)
SOUP	Amy's Kitchen Cream of Mushroom
CRACKERS	TLC Original 7-Grain (Kashi)
TORTILLAS	Sprouted Wheat Tortillas (Alvarado Street Bakery)
CHEESE ALTERNATIVE	Rice Shreds (Galaxy Foods)
BEANS	Eden Organic Black Beans (Eden Foods)
GINGER ALE	Reed's Ginger Brew (Reed's)
TORTILLA CHIPS	Sesame Blue Moons (Kettle)
SALSA	Frontera Classic Salsas (Frontera Foods)
SPELT FLOUR	Bob's Red Mill
TEMPEH	Organic Tempeh - Soy (Lightlife Foods)
TAHINI	Woodstock Farms
QUINOA	Bob's Red Mill
SOY SAUCE ALTERNATIVE	Bragg Liquid Aminos (Bragg Live Foods)
NUTRITIONAL YEAST	Red Star
FLAX OIL	Barlean's Organic Lignan Flaxseed Oil (Barlean's)
MISO	Miso Master (American Miso Company)
DULSE	Dulse Flakes (Maine Coast Sea Vegetables)

References

1. Jacobs, D.R., et al. "Editorial: It's more than an apple a day: an appropriately processed, plant-centered dietary pattern may be good for your health." *American Journal of Clinical Nutrition* 72 (2000):899–900.

2. Duke, J., Phytochemical and Ethnobotanical Database, http://www.ars-grin.gov/duke/

3. United States Department of Agriculture / Economic Research Service. "Total Chicken—Supply and Utilization." 2001.

4. Food & Drug Administration. "Risk Assessment of Fluoroquinolone Use in Poultry." February 2000.

5. Whole Foods Company. "Nationwide Survey Reveals Most Americans are Unaware They Consume Beef and Poultry Raised on Antibiotics." May 28, 2003. http://www.wholefoods.com/company/pr_05-28-03.html

6. Gupta, A., et al. Antimicrobial resistance among *Campylobacter* strains, U.S., 1997–2001. Emerging Infectious Diseases. 2004;10.

7. University of Nebraska-Lincoln Agricultural Research Division. Research Nebraska. September 2000.

8. Cherian, G., et al. "Fatty acid composition and egg components of specialty eggs." *Poultry Science* 81(2002): 30–3.

9. Hu, F.B., et al. "A prospective study of egg consumption and risk of cardiovascular disease in men and women." *Journal of the American Medical Association* 281(1999):1387–94.

10. Birch, E.E., et al. "Visual acuity and the essentiality of docosahexaenoic acid and arachidonic acid in the diet of term infants." *Pediatric Research* 44(1998):201–9.

11. FAO/WHO Expert Committee. "Fats and oils in human nutrition, food and nutrition." Paper No 57. FAO, Rome, Italy (1994).

12. United States Department of Agriculture National Agricultural Statistics Service. "Milk Cow Operations, 1993–2002, United States." USDA/NASS February, 2003.

13. United States Department of Agriculture National Agricultural Statistics Service. "Milk Production, 1994–2003, United States." USDA/NASS February, 2004.

14. LaDue, E., et al. "Future Structure of the Dairy Industry: Historical Trends, Projections and Issues." Cornell Program on Agricultural and Small Business Finance., R.B. 2003–01, June 2003, page 5.

15. United States Department of Agriculture National Agricultural Statistics Service. "Milk Per Cow 1994–2003, United States." USDA/NASS February, 2004.

16. Hebert, J.R., et al. "Nutritional and socioeconomic factors in relation to prostate cancer mortality: a cross-national study." *Journal of the National Cancer Institute* 90(1998): 1637–47.

17. Jacobsen, B.K., et al. "Does high soy milk intake reduce prostate cancer incidence? The Adventist Health Study (United States)." *Cancer Causes & Control* 9 (1998):553–7.

18. Hu, F.B., Stampfer, M.J. "Nut consumption and risk of coronary heart disease: a review of epidemiologic evidence." *Current Atherosclerosis Reports* 1(1999):204–9.

19. Shornikova, A.V., et al. "Lactobacillus reuteri as a therapeutic agent in acute diarrhea in young children." *Journal of Pediatric Gastroenterology and Nutrition* 24 (1997):399–404.

20. Moshfegh, A.J., et al. "Presence of inulin and oligofructose in the diets of Americans." *Journal of Nutrition* 129 (suppl)(1999):1407S–11S.

21. Appel, L.J., et al. "A clinical trial of the effects of dietary patterns on blood pressure." DASH Collaborative Research Group. *New England Journal of Medicine* 336 (1997):1117–24.

22. Jarvinen R., et al. "Prospective study on milk products, calcium and cancers of the colon and rectum." *European Journal of Clinical Nutrition* 55 (2001):1000–7.

23. Cox, C., et al. "Effects of dietary coconut oil, butter and safflower oil on plasma lipids, lipoproteins and lathosterol levels." *European Journal of Clinical Nutrition* 52 (1998):650–4.

24. Edem, D.O. "Palm oil: biochemical, physiological, nutritional, hematological, and toxicological aspects: a review." *Plant Foods for Human Nutrition* 57 (2002):319–41.

25. Elson, C.E. "Tropical oils: nutritional and scientific issues." *Critical Reviews in Food Science and Nutriton* 31 (1992):79–102.

26. Mensink, R.P., et al. "Effect of dietary trans fatty acids on serum lipids and lipoproteins: a meta-analysis of 27 trials." *Arteriosclerosis and Thrombosis* 56(1992):895–898.

27. Cleveland, L.E., et al. "Dietary intake of whole grains." *Journal of American College of Nutrition* 19 (suppl) (2000):331S–338S

28. Freudenheim, J.L., et al. "Risks associated with source of fiber and fiber components in cancer of the colon and rectum." *Cancer Research* 50 (1990): 3295–3300.

29. Spiller, G.A., et al. "Nuts and plasma lipids: an almond-based diet lowers LDL-C while preserving HDL-C." *Journal of the American College of Nutrition* 17 (1998): 285–90.

30. Sang S., et al. "Antioxidative phenolic compounds isolated from almond skins." *Journal of Agricultural and Food Chemistry* 50 (2002):2459–63.

31. Berges, R.R., et al. "Randomised, placebo-controlled, double-blind clinical trial of beta-sitosterol in patients with benign prostatic hyperplasia. Beta-sitosterol Study Group." *Lancet* 345 (1995):1529–32.

32. Slattery M.L., et al. "Plant foods, fiber, and rectal cancer." *American Journal of Clinical Nutrition* 79(2004):274–81.

33. Slattery M.L., et al. "Plant foods and colon cancer: an assessment of specific foods and their related nutrients (United States)." *Cancer Causes & Control.* 8(1997):575–90.

34. Salmeron, J., et al. "Dietary fiber, glycemic load, and risk of NIDDM in men." *Diabetes Care* 20 (1997):545–50.

35. Salmeron, J., et al. "Dietary fiber, glycemic load, and risk of non-insulin-dependent diabetes mellitus in women." *Journal of the American Medical Association* 277 (1997):472–7.

36. Wolk, A., et al. "Long-term intake of dietary fiber and decreased risk of coronary heart disease among women." *Journal of the American Medical Association* 281 (1999):1998–2004.

37. Liebman, B., Hurley, J. "The Juice Jungle." *Nutrition Action Newsletter* June 1999:13–15.

38. O'Byrne, D.J., et al. "Comparison of the antioxidant effects of Concord grape juice flavonoids alpha-tocopherol on markers of oxidative stress in healthy adults." *American Journal of Clinical Nutrition* 76(2002):1367–74.

39. Stacewicz-Sapuntzakis, M., et al. "Chemical composition and potential health effects of prunes: a functional food?" *Critical Review Food Science Nutrition* 41 (2001):251–86.

40. Ascherio, A., et al. "Intake of potassium, magnesium, calcium, and fiber and risk of stroke among US men." *Circulation* 98 (1998):1198–204.

41. Boato, F., et al. "Red grape juice inhibits iron availability: application of an in vitro digestion/caco-2 cell model." *Journal of Agricultural and Food Chemistry* 50 (2002): 6935–8.

42. Bazzano, L.A., et al. "Legume consumption and risk of coronary heart disease in US men and women: NHANES I Epidemiologic Follow-up Study." *Archives of Internal Medicine* 161 (2001):2573–8.

43. Beninger, C.W., et al. "Antioxidant activity of extracts, condensed tannin fractions, and pure flavonoids from Phaseolus vulgaris L. seed coat color genotypes." *Journal of Agricultural and Food Chemistry* 51 (2003):7879–83.

44. Ames, B.N. "DNA damage from micronutrient deficiencies is likely to be a major cause of cancer." *Mutation Research* 475 (2001):7–20.

45. Salmeron, J., et al. "Dietary fiber, glycemic load, and risk of NIDDM in men." *Diabetes Care* 20 (1997):545–50

46. Bray, et al., "Consumption of high-fructose corn syrup in beverages may play a role in the epidemic of obesity." *American Journal of Clinical Nutrition*, 79(2004):537–543.

47. Mahady, G.B., et al. "Ginger (Zingiber officinale Roscoe) and the gingerols inhibit the growth of Cag A+ strains of Helicobacter pylori." *Anticancer Research* 23 (2003):3699–702.

48. Vutyavanich, T., et al. "Ginger for nausea and vomiting in pregnancy: randomized, double-masked, placebo-controlled trial." *Obstetrics and Gynecology* 97 (2001):577–82.

49. Giovannucci, E. "Tomatoes, tomato-based products, lycopene, and cancer: review of the epidemiologic literature." *Journal of the National Cancer Institute* 91(1999): 317–31.

50. Levi, F., et al. "Dietary intake of selected micronutrients and breast-cancer risk." *International Journal of Cancer* 91 (2001):260–3.

51. Gann, P.H., et al. "Lower prostate cancer risk in men with elevated plasma lycopene levels: results of a prospective analysis." *Cancer Research* 59(1999):1225–30.

52. Chen, L., et al. "Oxidative DNA damage in prostate cancer patients consuming tomato sauce-based entrees as a whole-food intervention." *Journal of the National Cancer Institute* 93 (2001): 1872–9.

53. Kotake-Nara, E., et al. "Carotenoids affect proliferation of human prostate cancer cells." *Journal of Nutrition* 131 (2001):3303–6.

54. Steinberg, F.M., et al. "Soy protein with isoflavones has favorable effects on endothelial function that are independent of lipid and antioxidant effects in healthy postmenopausal women." *American Journal of Clinical Nutrition* 78 (2003):123–30.

55. Cooney, R.V., et al. "Effects of dietary sesame seeds on plasma tocopherol levels." *Nutrition and Cancer* 39 (2001):66–71.

56. Brenna, J.T. "Efficiency of conversion of alpha-linolenic acid to long chain n–3 fatty acids in man." *Current Opinion in Clinical Nutrition and Metabolic Care* 5(2002):127–32

57. Caughey, G.E., et al. "The effect on human tumor necrosis factor alpha and interleukin 1 beta production of diets enriched in n–3 fatty acids from vegetable oil or fish oil." *American Journal of Clinical Nutrition* 63 (1996):116–22.

58. Rallidis, L.S., et al. "Dietary alpha-linolenic acid decreases C-reactive protein, serum amyloid A and interleukin–6 in dyslipidaemic patients." *Atherosclerosis* 167 (2003):237–42.

59. Fukutake, M., et al. "Quantification of Genistein and Genistin in Soybeans and Soybean Products." *Food and Chemical Toxicology* 34 (1996): 457–61.

60. Ohara, M., et al. "Inhibition by long-term fermented miso of induction of gastric tumors by N-methyl-N′-nitro-N-nitrosoguanidine in CD (SD) rats." *Oncology Reports* 9 (2002):613–6.

61. Ohara, M., et al. "Prevention by long-term fermented miso of induction of colonic aberrant crypt foci by azoxymethane in F344 rats." *Oncology Reports* 9 (2002):69–73.

62. Shiraki, K., et al. "Inhibition by long-term fermented miso of induction of pulmonary adenocarcinoma by diisopropanolnitrosamine in Wistar rats." *Hiroshima Journal of Medical Sciences* 52 (2003):9–13.

63. Yamamoto, S., et al. "Soy, isoflavones, and breast cancer risk in Japan." *Journal of the National Cancer Institute* 95 (2003):906–13.

64. van Netten, C., et al. "Elemental and radioactive analysis of commercially available seaweed." *The Science of the Total Environment* 255 (2000): 169–75.

65. Hollowell, J.G., et al. "Iodine nutrition in the United States. Trends and public health implications: iodine excretion data from National Health and Nutrition Examination Surveys I and III (1971–1974 and 1988–1994)." *Journal of Clinical Endocrinology & Metabolism* 83 (1998):3401–8.

66. Pennington, J.A. "A review of iodine toxicity reports." *Journal of the American Dietetic Association* 90 (1990):1571–81.

67. Cann, S.A., et al. "Hypothesis: iodine, selenium and the development of breast cancer." *Cancer Causes & Control* 11 (2000):121–7.

68. Funahashi, H., et al. "Wakame seaweed suppresses the proliferation of 7,12-dimethylbenz(a)-anthracene-induced mammary tumors in rats." *Japanese Journal of Cancer Research* 90 (1999):922–7.

69. Funahashi, H., et al. "Seaweed prevents breast cancer?" *Japanese Journal of Cancer Research* 92(2001):483–7.

70. Mead, P.S., et al. "Food-Related Illness and Death in the United States." *Emerging Infectious Diseases* 5(1999):607–625.

71. Phillips, I., et al. "Does the Use of Antibiotics in Food Animals Pose a Risk to Human Health?" *Animal Health Institute*, January, 2004.

72. Cornell University Program on Breast Cancer and Environmental Risk Factors in New York State. June 2000; Fact Sheet #37.

73. Holmes, M.D., et al. "Dietary correlates of plasma insulin-like growth factor I and insulin-like growth factor binding protein 3 concentrations." Cancer *Epidemiology Biomarkers & Prevention* 11 (2002):852–61.

74. Hollander, D. "Intestinal permeability, leaky gut, and intestinal disorders." *Current Gastroenterology Reports* 1 (1999):410–6.

75. Simon, S. (2004, January 4). "Mad Cow Case Casts Light on Beef Uses." *The Los Angeles Times*, pp. A1.

76. *Render Magazine*, December 2001.

77. Eduljee, G.H., et al. "Validation of a methodology for modeling PCDD and PCDF intake via the food chain." *Science of the Total Environment* 183 (1996):211–29.

78. U.S. Environmental Protection Agency. "Exposure and Human Health Reassessment of 2,3,7,8-Tetrachlorodibenzo-p-dioxin (TCDD) and Related Compounds." EPA/ 600/P–00/001Ac. May 2000.

79. Worthington, V. "Nutritional Quality of Organic Versus Conventional Fruits, Vegetables, and Grains." *The Journal of Alternative and Complimentary Medicine* 7 (2001):161–73.

80. Center for Science in the Public Interest. "A Guide to Food Additives." *Nutrition Action Newsletter.* March 1999: 4–9.

81. Appel L.J., et al. "A clinical trial of the effects of dietary patterns on blood pressure." DASH Collaborative Research Group. *New England Journal of Medicine* 336 (1997):1117–24.

82. Swagerty, D.L., et al. "Lactose intolerance." *American Family Physician* 65 (2002):1845–50.

83. Host, A., et al. "The natural history of cow's milk protein allergy/intolerance." *European Journal of Clinical Nutrition* 49 (suppl) (1995):S13–8.

84. Oranje A.P., et al. "Natural course of cow's milk allergy in childhood atopic eczema/dermatitis syndrome." *Annals of Allergy, Asthma and Immunology* 6 (suppl) (2002):52–5.

85. Sbarbati A., et al. "Gluten sensitivity and 'normal' histology: is the intestinal mucosa really normal?" *Digestive and Liver Disease* 11(2003):768–73.

86. Not T., et al. "Celiac disease risk in the USA: high prevalence of antiendomysium antibodies in healthy blood donors." *Scandinavian Journal of Gastroenterology* 33 (1998):494–8.

87. Anderson R.L., "Compositional changes in trypsin inhibitors, phytic acid, saponins and isoflavones related to soybean processing." *Journal of Nutrition* (3 suppl) 125(1995):581S–588S.

88. Mensink, R.P., et al. "Effects of dietary fatty acids and carbohydrates on the ratio of serum total to HDL cholesterol and on serum lipids and apolipoproteins: a meta-analysis of 60 controlled trials." *American Journal of Clinical Nutrition* 77(2003):1146–55.

89. Sun CQ, et al. "Antibacterial actions of fatty acids and monoglycerides against Helicobacter pylori." *FEMS Immunology and Medical Microbiology* 36 (2003):9–17.

90. Edem, D.O. "Palm oil: biochemical, physiological, nutritional, hematological, and toxicological aspects: a review." *Plant Foods for Human Nutrition* 57 (2002):319–41.

91. Pischon T., et al. "Habitual dietary intake of n–3 and n–6 fatty acids in relation to inflammatory markers among US men and women." *Circulation* 108 (2003):155–60.

92. Caughey, G.E., et al. "The effect on human tumor necrosis factor alpha and interleukin–1 beta production of diets enriched in n–3 fatty acids from vegetable oil or fish oil." *American Journal of Clinical Nutrition* 63 (1996):116–22.

93. Keys, A. "Coronary heart disease in seven countries." *Circulation* 41 (suppl 1) (1970):S1–211.

94. Hu, F.B., Stampfer, M.J. "Nut consumption and risk of coronary heart disease: a review of epidemiologic evidence." *Current Atherosclerosis Reports* 1 (1999):204–9.

Index

Information About the Author

In addition to working as the nutritionist for the Duke Center for Integrative Medicine, Greg Hottinger works in private practice in Asheville, NC. He counsels individuals on creating a diet designed to restore and/or maintain optimal health. He also teaches classes and speaks to groups about healthy eating. For information regarding individual phone consults or speaking engagements, visit www.hippiefood.com or email Greg@hippiefood.com.

Greg has also co-created a successful weight-loss program that he coaches by phone on an individual basis. For information regarding this program and wellness coaching, visit www.novowellness.com or email Greg@novowellness.com.

Order Form

ON-LINE ORDERS: www.hippiefood.com
MAIL ORDERS: Huckleberry Mountain Press
                  P.O. Box 8651
                  Asheville, NC 28814 USA

PRODUCT	QUANTITY	PRICE	SUBTOTAL
The Best Natural Foods on the Market Today: A Yuppie's Guide to Hippie Food, Volume I	_____	$14.95	_____
Shipping ($3.00 for 1st book/$2.00 for each additional book)			_____
Sales tax (7% NC residents)			_____
TOTAL			_____

Name: _____

Address: _____

City / ST / Zip: _____

Phone number: _____

Email address: _____

Ship to: ❑ Address above

Name: _____

Address: _____

City / ST / Zip: _____

Payment:
❑ Check ❑ Visa ❑ MasterCard

Card Number: _____

Name on Card: _____

Expiration date: _____

Signature: _____

THE BEST NATURAL FOODS
on the Market Today

A Yuppie's Guide
to Hippie Food
Volume 1

www.hippiefood.com

Manufacturer's Coupon | Expires 12/31/05

SAVE 50¢ OFF ANY
Woodstock Farms Almond Butter Product

20401

www.knudsenjuices.com

MANUFACTURER'S COUPON
EXPIRES DECEMBER 31, 2005
DO NOT DOUBLE

132282

MANUFACTURER COUPON   EXPIRES 12/31/05

Save 55¢ Now!
on any HORIZON ORGANIC product

Good on one (1) **HORIZON ORGANIC** product.

Creamy Cultured Soy
SAVE 25¢
on ANY 6 OZ. CUP

Save 50¢
on any variety Eden bean

EDEN.
www.edenfoods.com

Great Taste and Nutritious!

SOYCO SOYCO **FOODS**

Rice® Products are always:
Soy Free
Lactose & Cholesterol Free
Low Fat (Trans Fatty Acid Free)
Gluten Free

1g Total Carb per serving
6g Protein

NATURAL INGREDIENTS

SUPER NATURAL FLAVOR™

75¢ OFF
all
8OZ KETTLE™ BRAND TORTILLA CHIPS

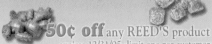